Where You Are

Where You Are

Kristen Da Silva

SCIROCCO DRAMA

Where You Are
first published 2022 by Scirocco Drama
An imprint of J. Gordon Shillingford Publishing Inc.
© 2022 Kristen Da Silva

Scirocco Drama Editor: Glenda MacFarlane
Cover design by Doowah Design
Author photo by Patrick Hodgson
Production photos by Sharyn Ayliffe

Printed and bound in Canada on 100% post-consumer recycled paper.
We acknowledge the financial support of the Manitoba Arts Council and
The Canada Council for the Arts for our publishing program.

Production inquiries to:
Colin Rivers, Managing Literary Agent
Marquis Entertainment Inc.
73 Richmond St West, Suite #312
Toronto, ON M5H 4E8
info@mqlit.ca

Library and Archives Canada Cataloguing in Publication

Title: Where you are / Kristen Da Silva.
Names: Da Silva, Kristen, author.
Description: A play.
Identifiers: Canadiana (print) 20220196281 | Canadiana (ebook) 2022019629X |
ISBN 9781927922941 (softcover) | ISBN 9781990737107 (HTML)
Classification: LCC PS8607.A22 W54 2022 | DDC C812/.6—dc23

J. Gordon Shillingford Publishing
P.O. Box 86, RPO Corydon Avenue, Winnipeg, MB Canada R3M 3S3
www.jgshillingford.com

For Aunt Ruth

Kristen Da Silva

Kristen Da Silva was born in Oakville, Ontario and raised in Nobleton, Ontario, a small farming community in King Township. She graduated from York University and continued her studies at Sheridan College.

Her plays, which include *Sugar Road, Where You Are, Hurry Hard, The Rules of Playing Risk* and *Beyond the Sea,* are set in Ontario locales from Sudbury to Stayner and have been produced in provinces across Canada and in the United States. She is a two-time recipient of the Playwrights Guild New Comedy award.

She currently lives in Oakville and works as a writer and actor. She is the mother of three children, Luke, Virginia, and Jude.

Acknowledgments

Dr. Jane Healey, Colin Rivers and the team at Marquis Literary, Norm Foster, Diane Horner, Michael Anania, Esther Chung, Ryk Simpson and Lindsay Osborne.

The artists, designers, crew and administrators at Theatre Orangeville, where this play premiered, with special thanks to Artistic Director David Nairn and the cast: Melanie Janzen, Debra Hale and Jeff Hanson.

My loves, Nelson, Luke, Virginia and Jude.

Foreword
by David Nairn

I read dozens and dozens of scripts every year, as play development and the selection of plays for inclusion in our season playbill form perhaps the most integral (and fun!) part of what I do as an artistic director.

Rarely, if you're very lucky, a play crosses your path that quite literally makes you catch your breath, fixate on it until you've devoured reading it for the fourth time in that very first sitting, and immediately sets your imagination on fire.

For me, most recently, that gem of a play was *Where You Are*.

Having spent a great deal of time myself in a community very similar to the one in which the play is set, I couldn't help but be drawn into Kristen's world, a world populated by wonderful characters, every one of whom I still think of as a dear friend.

As we worked together towards her final refinement of the script, through the creation of the world premiere production, Kristen's writing and her approach to her writing never failed to inspire me as a director.

I read somewhere once that what brings people into the theatre are great stories that are relevant to them; stories that are fiercely original, bravely vulnerable, passionately told and honest to the last word.

Without doubt, that is true of *Where You Are*.

To spend time in the world of this play brings you where you want to be, where you are, for as long as you're lucky enough to be there.

December 2021

David Nairn is the Artistic Director of Theatre Orangeville.

Patrick (Jeff Hanson) visits with Glenda (Melanie Janzen) and
Suzanne (Debra Hale).

Mother-daughter tensions mount between Beth (Kristen Da Silva)
and Suzanne (Debra Hale) while Glenda (Melanie Janzen) attempts to
mediate.

Glenda (Melanie Janzen) comforts Beth (Kristen Da Silva) while Suzanne (Debra Hale) looks on.

Patrick (Jeff Hanson) meets Beth (Kristen Da Silva).

Beth (Kristen Da Silva) gives a sobriety test to Glenda (Melanie Janzen) and Suzanne (Debra Hale).

Patrick (Jeff Hanson) accompanies Beth (Kristen Da Silva) home from a wedding.

Production History

Where You Are was first produced by Theatre Orangeville in May 2019 with the following creative team:

GLENDA .... Melanie Janzen

SUZANNE .... Debra Hale

BETH .... Kristen Da Silva

PATRICK .... Jeff Hanson

Director .... David Nairn

Set Design .... Beckie Morris

Lighting Design .... Wendy Lundgren

Costume Design .... Wendi Speck

Stage Manager .... Jory McLean

Apprentice Stage Manager .... Grace Batten

Characters

GLENDA

In her fifties, the owner of the home.

SUZANNE

In her fifties, lives with her sister GLENDA.

BETH

In her thirties, SUZANNE's daughter, a doctor.

PATRICK

In his thirties, the neighbour, a veterinarian.

Setting

The front porch and yard of the Beaton family home, in Little Current on Manitoulin Island. The porch is well-appointed, with comfortable chairs, a table which presently holds a tray with two cups, a pot of coffee and a radio. There are crates of jam stacked in one corner and various pots of flowers about. In the yard there is a small gazebo or arbour over a garden bench. Summer.

ACT ONE

Scene One

The present. Summer. Early afternoon.

The sound of chickens. Lights up. SUZANNE enters from the house in a housecoat. Her hair is very messy. She has smudged makeup on from the day before.

SUZANNE: Bloody noisy chickens, what do you want?! What can I do for you? How do I satisfy whatever it is that makes you bellow endlessly day and night like tiny, winged beasts from the depths of hell?

GLENDA enters from the side of the house. She carries an empty wood crate.

GLENDA: You calling me?

SUZANNE: No, I'm not calling you. I was swearing at the chickens.

GLENDA: Well, you're probably wasting your breath, I suspect very few of them speak English. Good to see you up.

SUZANNE: Good morning.

GLENDA: Morning still ends at noon, Suzanne.

SUZANNE: Well, it's morning somewhere.

GLENDA: Yes, well, here on Manitoulin Island it's twelve-thirty. *(Beat.)* This is a good look.

SUZANNE: What?

GLENDA: You look like the front man of a heavy metal band.

SUZANNE: No, I don't.

GLENDA: You look like a porcupine with a serious drug habit.

SUZANNE: Glenda.

GLENDA: No, you know what you look like? You look like Uncle Leonard when he got struck by lightning on Halloween.

SUZANNE: I didn't sleep well, thank you very much.

GLENDA: No, I can see that. There's coffee there.

SUZANNE: Thank you.

SUZANNE pours herself a coffee.

GLENDA: Want to talk about it?

SUZANNE: What?

GLENDA: What's bothering you.

SUZANNE: Nothing's bothering me. *(Beat.)* Why did we get those chickens? I hate them. Especially that one with the hairdo.

GLENDA: The rooster?

SUZANNE: Yes. The rooster. Every morning. *(She crows like a rooster.)* So proud to be the first one up. You know what? I'm not impressed. He only works for thirty seconds a day. And I don't need an animal to wake me up. You know what I need? An animal that will do my taxes. Get me one of those. I don't need a rooster, because I have an alarm clock that eats less, and it has a snooze button!

GLENDA:	Is this why you were up all night? You don't like the rooster's work ethic?
SUZANNE:	No.
GLENDA:	Then what's really on your mind?
SUZANNE:	I don't know. Nothing.
GLENDA:	I'm just gonna spitball then...Is this about Beth coming home?
SUZANNE:	No. Why would it be? She's my daughter. I'm looking forward to her coming home. *(Beat.)* What?
GLENDA:	I don't know, maybe you're reflecting on how much you two argued last time?
SUZANNE:	No. I'm not reflecting on anything. And we didn't argue that much.
GLENDA:	I've seen productions of *King Lear* with less conflict.
SUZANNE:	Oh, please.
GLENDA:	Suzanne. We were both here. *(Beat.)* Look, if you want it to be different this time, maybe it's simple.
SUZANNE:	Is it?
GLENDA:	Yeah. You know, I was thinking, maybe whatever you feel like saying, just don't.
SUZANNE:	What?
GLENDA:	When you want to say something to Beth, don't.
SUZANNE:	Don't say anything, that's your suggestion? I'll just sit here silently for a week?

GLENDA: No, but maybe when you have a critical thought, instead of voicing it, you could do something else.

SUZANNE: Like what?

GLENDA: I don't know, whistle.

SUZANNE: Whistle? Like the dwarves from *Snow White?*

GLENDA: They seemed to get along.

SUZANNE: That's ridiculous. Anyway, I'm not critical. How is it you've decided I'm the reason Beth and I bicker?

GLENDA: You're at least fifty percent of the reason.

SUZANNE: Well, it takes two to tango. And she starts it.

GLENDA: Now, see? She's not even here yet and you're already bickering with her. And by the look of you, you went ten rounds with her last night, too. Look, I love you both and I know you love each other. It's not complicated. Just be nice. Give her a compliment. Tell her you're glad she's here.

SUZANNE: Fine.

GLENDA: Don't be pushy, give her space.

SUZANNE: Okay.

GLENDA: Don't ask prying questions.

SUZANNE: What's a prying question? I'm not allowed to ask questions?

GLENDA: You can ask questions. "Would you like another piece of toast?" is fine. "Who are sleeping with?" is prying.

SUZANNE: Got it.

GLENDA: Good. *(Beat.)* And maybe you should start washing your face before you go to bed.

SUZANNE: I'm going to wash it. Is it okay with you if I have my morning coffee first?

GLENDA: Only if that coffee can time travel.

                        Beat.

SUZANNE: What about you? What are you all dressed up for?

GLENDA: I was at church.

SUZANNE: Church?

GLENDA: Yeah, church.

SUZANNE: Since when do you go to church?

GLENDA: I've been to church plenty of times.

SUZANNE: Only because that's where they hold the bake sale.

GLENDA: Suzanne, I can go to church. I can be very churchly. Sometimes I'm downright pious. You know, Dad took us to church when we were girls.

SUZANNE: He took us once, because someone died.

GLENDA: So? We went.

SUZANNE: All right. Which church did you go to?

GLENDA: Why do you ask?

SUZANNE: I'm just curious which religion we are.

GLENDA: I went to the pretty one.

SUZANNE: The pretty one.

GLENDA: Yes.

SUZANNE: Holy Trinity?

GLENDA: Is that the pretty one?

SUZANNE: Did you walk all that way?

GLENDA: Oh, I've got to make a note that we're out of blueberry. I sold the last jar this morning to a couple from Vaughan.

SUZANNE: Glenda—

GLENDA: You wouldn't believe how they spell that. There's a silent g.

SUZANNE: Glenda. That's too far.

GLENDA: The alpacas were out. I don't care what George says, there is something wrong with that little one.

SUZANNE: You're supposed to be doing less.

GLENDA: He walked straight into the fence post. He's either dim-witted or he needs alpaca glasses.

SUZANNE: Hey! Stop ignoring me.

GLENDA: Stop worrying about me.

SUZANNE: I'm just saying—

GLENDA: Worry about yourself! You look like you've got rabies!

SUZANNE: I'm just reminding you—

GLENDA: You think I need reminding? I don't need reminding. I wake up every morning with pain that wasn't there a year ago and I'm reminded. I walk up our hill—a hill I've been walking up for years but now I get winded three steps up—and I'm reminded. I don't need you reminding me.

SUZANNE: Okay.

GLENDA: And, while we're on the subject, I'm not taking any more of those vitamins you bought. They give me indigestion.

SUZANNE: I read on the internet—

GLENDA: I'm not doing something just because you read it on the internet!

SUZANNE: Okay.

GLENDA: So stop. Stop reading. Stop fussing. Stop worrying.

SUZANNE: Well…I can't. But I can do a better job keeping it to myself. *(Beat.)* Okay? Truce? Please?

GLENDA: Yeah…well…comb your hair.

SUZANNE: Truce!

GLENDA: Fine. Truce.

> *SUZANNE pats her hair down. There's a silence while they let the conflict die.*

SUZANNE: How was it, anyway, church? What's the gossip?

GLENDA: Suzanne, I didn't go to get gossip. *(Beat.)* No, I can't even say that with a straight face. You know how I told you I think Walt Kelly is involved in a secret love affair?

SUZANNE: Yeah, because he bought new jeans.

GLENDA: Exactly. Well, listen to this. He showed up this morning wearing hair gel.

SUZANNE:	Hair gel!
GLENDA:	He was practically shellacked.
SUZANNE:	Wow. Who do you think that's for?
GLENDA:	What, do you think I'm an amateur? I know who it's for.
SUZANNE:	Well, don't keep me in suspense.
GLENDA:	Andrea Faulkner. She's from Espanola.
SUZANNE:	A bi-coastal relationship! How'd you figure it out?
GLENDA:	Because she was in church this morning! Now I ask you, is there not a single church in Espanola?
SUZANNE:	There's gotta be at least one.
GLENDA:	That's right. But there she was. And when Walt was looking for a place to sit, don't you want to bet that Andy just happened to have a spot right next to her.
SUZANNE:	Of course she did.
GLENDA:	They shared a hymnal. If that doesn't have tawdry sex written all over it, I don't know what does.
SUZANNE:	Sex before marriage. What will people say?
GLENDA:	I mean, he is sixty-eight.
SUZANNE:	I wonder what he's like in bed.
GLENDA:	Well, don't picture it.
SUZANNE:	Too late. Quick, tell me something else. I need a palate cleanser.
GLENDA:	Oh, here comes one now.

SUZANNE and GLENDA look across the yard as PATRICK enters. He has a newspaper.

PATRICK: Afternoon.

SUZANNE/
GLENDA: Patrick!/Hello!

PATRICK: Got your newspaper again.

SUZANNE: Again?

GLENDA: That paper boy is lazy. He just hurls it from the car window.

SUZANNE: I don't think you can call him a paper *boy*. He's nearly thirty. Thanks for bringing it over, Patrick.

SUZANNE takes the paper.

PATRICK: It's no trouble. I wouldn't want you to miss out on the news.

SUZANNE: Yes. Goodness. What hijinks are the locals up to today? Oh, look. Someone's garbage cans were broken into. *(Reading further, she gasps.)* They suspect raccoons.

GLENDA: Patrick, can I interest you in some iced tea?

PATRICK: Oh no, I was just bringing the paper over. I've got to get back—

SUZANNE: Oh, surely you have a few minutes to spare for the town spinsters.

GLENDA: Hey. I'm not a spinster. I'm a widow.

SUZANNE: She's a widow.

PATRICK: I would love to, truly, but—

SUZANNE: We have homemade pound cake.

PATRICK: Do you?

GLENDA: Do we?

SUZANNE: Yes, we do. Baked fresh today. I was up with
                the roosters.

PATRICK: Well, that sounds great, but—

SUZANNE: You're not going to say no? I've been sweating
                all morning over a hot stove.

GLENDA: *(To SUZANNE.)* Oven.

SUZANNE: Oven. A hot oven.

GLENDA: Look, she didn't even have time to comb her
                hair or wash her face.

SUZANNE: Did wash my hands though.

PATRICK: Well, good, but to be honest with you,
                Suzanne, I've had a little too much cake lately.

GLENDA: Still making your way through that, huh?

PATRICK: Yeah. Turns out wedding cake for two
                hundred people lasts a long time when
                you're the only one eating it.

GLENDA: Maybe it would have been better to throw it
                out, all things considered?

PATRICK: Throw it out? No, ma'am. That cake cost me
                nine hundred dollars.

GLENDA: Nine hundred dollars!

SUZANNE: They sure saw you coming.

PATRICK: Yup. So I'm choking down every last bite
                of it. Even those little flowers that taste like
                toothpaste.

SUZANNE: Tina didn't want any of it?

PATRICK: No. No! She's vegan now...because of Chad.

Each time PATRICK says Chad's name it sounds like a swear word.

SUZANNE: He's vegan?

PATRICK: Yeah.

SUZANNE: But he's a butcher.

PATRICK: Yep. He's a vegan butcher, Chad is. Ridiculous, isn't it? Not as ridiculous as his haircut, though, or his...stupid face. *(Beat.)* Yeah, all right. I'll have some pound cake.

SUZANNE: All right! You just sit your tight little...self down and I'll bring it out.

GLENDA: *(Sotto, as SUZANNE passes.)* Don't forget to take it out of the package.

SUZANNE: *(Sotto.)* This isn't the first time I've entertained a man, Glenda. *(To PATRICK.)* Be right back!

SUZANNE exits to the house.

PATRICK: I'm sorry about that. I guess I'm still working through some stuff there.

GLENDA: Oh, honey, if you need a safe place to say bad things about people, you've found it.

PATRICK: Thank you.

GLENDA: We know you don't mean it. You're just blowing off steam.

PATRICK: I'm not imposing, am I? I feel like every time I pop by, you kind ladies end up running around serving me things.

GLENDA: Of course you're not. We love when you come to visit, with your stories, and the rest of you.

PATRICK: You know, I'm out of jam.

GLENDA: You are? Well, we can't have that. Raspberry, right?

PATRICK: Yep…That's my jam. *(He takes out his wallet.)* How much does a jar go for these days?

GLENDA: Well, five dollars for a local, twelve for a tourist. They seem to feel better about what they're buying when it's expensive. I can't figure it out. *(She turns and sees him with his wallet out.)* Now, I told you before, Patrick Davies, I don't want your money.

PATRICK: I insist.

GLENDA: I won't hear of it.

PATRICK: Well, I don't feel right just taking it.

GLENDA: We're just talking about a jar of jam, Patrick. I'm not giving you a kidney.

PATRICK: I hate to take advantage of your kindness.

GLENDA: What's a little jam between neighbours?

PATRICK: I suppose.

GLENDA: And I don't want anything in return, either.

PATRICK: Well, that's very good of you.

GLENDA: Nothing. We're neighbours. This is what neighbours do.

PATRICK: Then I count myself lucky to have a neighbour like you.

GLENDA: I mean it. You don't owe me a thing. There's no debt. Your ledger is clear.

PATRICK: Thank you.

GLENDA: All right, well, I can see from your face that you're feeling guilty about it and we can't have that. Would you like to reroof my shed?

PATRICK: Oh.

GLENDA: Normally I'd do it myself, but—

PATRICK: Say no more. I can help.

GLENDA: No rush. Anytime this week is fine.

PATRICK: This week?

GLENDA: You're not too busy, are you?

PATRICK: Well, I…I'm sure I can fit it in.

GLENDA: It is so nice of you to offer!

PATRICK: Did I?

                SUZANNE enters with cake on a plate and a pitcher of iced tea.

SUZANNE: Suzanne's famous pound cake!

GLENDA: Suzanne, Patrick has just offered to reroof the shed.

SUZANNE: Patrick, you are a prince among men.

PATRICK: Well, I know how uncomfortable standing out in the sun doing manual labour is.

SUZANNE: Here we go…

PATRICK: That looks delicious. Just a sliver for me.

SUZANNE: You sure?

PATRICK: Yes, thank you. Just a tiny piece. *(SUZANNE serves him a massive piece of cake.)* Yep, that's perfect.

SUZANNE: All right. Don't be shy if you want seconds. *(Beat.)* Now, how are things for you, Patrick? Now that your mouth is full, tell us all the trials and tribulations of a country vet.

PATRICK: Oh, it's all pretty good, thanks.

GLENDA: I heard you were over at Kendall Cranford's farm.

PATRICK: Yes, that's true.

SUZANNE: Old Kendall Cranford.

GLENDA: Suzanne went out with him once.

SUZANNE: Most stimulating night of my life. Told me the full history of the Holstein.

GLENDA: It couldn't have been that bad. You got in at six a.m.

SUZANNE: Yes, I had to sleep with him to shut him up.

         PATRICK chokes a bit on his cake.

GLENDA: So, you were over at Kendall's?

PATRICK: Yeah. I was over there today. I was inseminating a cow.

SUZANNE: That's going a bit above and beyond, isn't it, Doc?

PATRICK: What? Oh, no! I didn't mean I was…I had to help because Kendall had his hip replaced so he's not up to the task, himself. *(Beat.)* Noo. I am phrasing this badly.

GLENDA: She's just teasing you, Patrick. Don't listen to her. Go on, this is fascinating. How exactly do you inseminate a cow?

PATRICK: Well, that's not really an iced tea and cake kind of conversation.

SUZANNE: Now, you see, that whole thing strikes me as a shame. I mean, sex has to be one of the few highlights in a cow's life. You can't let them get it done the old-fashioned way?

PATRICK: Sometimes it's not that easy.

SUZANNE: Sure it is. Wait until dusk, stick 'em in a pen together and put on some Michael Bublé.

PATRICK: The fact of the matter is, Kendall's bull was having a little trouble...performing.

SUZANNE: Ah. Like father, like son.

GLENDA: Are you blushing, Doc?

PATRICK: Noo.

SUZANNE: What's there to blush about over here? He spent all morning with his arm up a cow's hoo-ha. *(To PATRICK.)* Have some more iced tea.

PATRICK: Thank you.

GLENDA: Change of subject?

PATRICK: Please.

GLENDA: We heard a strange rumour about you.

PATRICK: Am I going to like this subject any better?

GLENDA: About Tina's upcoming nuptials.

PATRICK: Oh...

SUZANNE:	We were told you're going.
GLENDA:	You're not going, are you? That would be crazy.
PATRICK:	Well, I'm not going myself, per se. I'm sort of going as someone else's escort.
SUZANNE:	Who?
PATRICK:	Sparky.
SUZANNE:	Who the hell is Sparky?
PATRICK:	He's a border collie. Tina and I adopted him when he was a puppy. Now we have joint custody.
SUZANNE:	Of the dog?
PATRICK:	Yeah.
GLENDA:	She wants the dog at the wedding?
PATRICK:	He's the ring bearer.
GLENDA:	And you're going to bring him?
PATRICK:	Well, it lands on my weekend.
GLENDA:	Are you sure that's a good idea, Patrick? I can't imagine it'll be easy to watch her exchange vows with vegan Chad so soon after she left you at the altar.
PATRICK:	She didn't exactly leave me *at* the altar. I was still at the hotel.
GLENDA:	My apologies. She left you *near* the altar.

PATRICK: Yeah. *(Beat.)* I know it sounds absurd but, for all the things you can say about her, she does love that dog. And my therapist said the best way to exorcise your demons is to stare 'em in the eye. So, that's what I'm doing. *(Beat.)* Not that Tina is a demon.

SUZANNE: No, you couldn't go that far.

GLENDA: Suzanne. *(Beat.)* Actually, Patrick, I think it's very noble of you.

PATRICK: You do?

GLENDA: Yes. Are you bringing a date? I mean a human one.

PATRICK: I certainly implied I was. *(Beat.)* You know that little box on the RSVP where you indicate how many people are in your party? I wrote "Two." I don't know what came over me. At first I wrote "One." Then I stared at it…and it looked so pathetic. I mean, in the year since we split up, she's managed to meet, fall in love with and get engaged to someone else. And me? I'm bringing a border collie to her wedding. Actually, technically he's bringing me.

GLENDA: So you don't have a date, then?

PATRICK: Not yet.

GLENDA: Well, you're cutting it a little close, aren't you? The wedding's on Saturday.

PATRICK: Yeah…What are you doing Saturday?

GLENDA: We're going to the wedding.

PATRICK: You are? I didn't know you liked Tina.

GLENDA: Oh, we don't. No, we're going for her mom, Deb. She did a lot for me when my husband Mark died. So, we'll be there. We just haven't figured out what we're going to do with Beth yet. She's coming home for a visit this week.

PATRICK: *(To SUZANNE.)* Your daughter?

SUZANNE: Yes.

GLENDA: We'll have to introduce you! You'll love her. She's a real smart cookie. Went to school on full scholarships. She gets that from me. *(SUZANNE gives GLENDA a look.)* What? I was class valedictorian.

SUZANNE: Only because Lenny Thompson got mono and couldn't give the speech.

GLENDA: That's not why.

SUZANNE: I can tell you one thing, she didn't get her brains from her father.

PATRICK: Your ex-husband?

SUZANNE: No, God no. We never married. I only knew him briefly, which was enough time to tell he wasn't a Nobel laureate.

PATRICK: I see.

SUZANNE: You have to understand, back then I was somewhat of a footloose kind of person.

GLENDA: Back then?

SUZANNE: You know, it was the time of free love.

GLENDA: Suzanne, it was the eighties.

SUZANNE: Anyway, he wasn't that interested in being a father, and I wasn't that interested in being a wife. He did write a song about me, called "Suzanne." It wasn't quite as good as the one by Leonard Cohen, if you're wondering. No, the best thing he gave me was Beth. And she's coming for a visit.

GLENDA: You be sure to pop over when she gets here, okay?

PATRICK: Of course. I'd love to meet her. Well, I better get back to it. There's a litter of sheep dogs down on Boosneck Road I promised I'd check in on.

                He sets his cake down. He's eaten only a fraction.

SUZANNE: You didn't like the cake I laboured over?

PATRICK: It's not that…it's just you gave me such a big piece. Maybe I could eat it in installments?

SUZANNE: I'll put it in the fridge.

PATRICK: Thank you. Have a good day.

GLENDA: You too, Patrick.

                PATRICK exits.

GLENDA: Now, there goes the salt of the earth. I don't know what is up with Tina Forester. That is the sort of man you don't let go of.

SUZANNE: Oh, I'd hold on to him for dear life.

                End of scene.

Scene Two

Early evening.

Lights up. The coffee has been replaced with a pitcher of punch. The sound of angry chickens. BETH enters, backing in. She is dressed conservatively, in a blouse and khaki pants. She has her keys in her hand and is holding them out in self-defence. She pulls a rolling suitcase and calls back to a chicken, offstage.

BETH: Whoa whoa whoa! Stay! No. No! Shoo! What is wrong with you? *(Without taking her eyes off the chicken.)* Aunt Glenda?! Mom?!

GLENDA enters from the house, wiping her hands on a dish towel.

GLENDA: Beth?

BETH: Hi!

GLENDA: What's wrong?

BETH: It followed me from my car!

GLENDA: What did?

BETH: That chicken!

GLENDA: Oh.

BETH: It's looking at me like it wants to kill me.

GLENDA snaps her dish towel at the chicken.

GLENDA: Go on! Get outta here. *(To BETH.)* I'm sorry, honey. You'll have to forgive her. She's been pretty riled up today.

BETH: What the hell is wrong with her?

GLENDA: We just ate her sister. *(To the chicken, snapping the dish towel again.)* I mean it. Go on now, Joanne. I've got a deep fryer in there with your name on it. That's right, back to the coop with you. Go do something productive. Lay some eggs or something. *(To BETH.)* You okay?

BETH: Yeah. *(Beat.)* Joanne?

GLENDA: We name them all after people in town we don't like. Makes killing 'em easier. *(Beat.)* Well, come on! Bring it in!

BETH: Hi!

BETH and GLENDA embrace with affection.

GLENDA: I can't believe you're finally here! And look at you! Just look at you! Look at your boobies!

BETH: Aunt Glenda.

GLENDA: *(Hollering.)* Suzanne! Beth's here! *(To BETH.)* How was the drive?

BETH: Not bad once I got out of the city. *(Beat.)* You look thinner.

GLENDA: Oh, do I? Well, must be all the walking I do. It is so good to have you home. How have you been?

BETH: Good. Fine. How have you been?

GLENDA: Great! Everything's great. You look good. I could just eat you up! *(Beat. Hollering.)* Suzanne! Beth's here! Come see her boobies!

BETH: Aunt Glenda, I'm a grown woman. I'd appreciate if you didn't stand in the front yard yelling about my boobies.

GLENDA: They're so upright, aren't they? You enjoy those. *(Hollering.)* Suzanne!

> *SUZANNE enters. She has cleaned herself up and changed. Her dress might be described as "bohemian."*

There you are! What did you do, put on lipstick?

BETH: Mom!

SUZANNE: Beth!

> *SUZANNE and BETH hug. It lacks the abandon of the hug between GLENDA and BETH.*

GLENDA: Oh, it's so good to have us all back together! *(In SUZANNE's ear, sotto.)* Remember: compliment.

BETH: What?

GLENDA: Nothing.

SUZANNE: *(To BETH.)* You're here!

BETH: Yes.

SUZANNE: And you're…wearing pants.

BETH: Yes.

SUZANNE: And you grew your hair.

BETH: Yeah, a bit.

SUZANNE: Got a new suitcase.

BETH: Yep?

> *BETH crosses to collect her suitcase from the yard.*

GLENDA:	(*Sotto.*) Those are not compliments, those are just statements of fact!
SUZANNE:	(*Sotto.*) I'm trying!
GLENDA:	(*Sotto.*) Try harder! Tell her you like what she's wearing.
SUZANNE:	(*Sotto.*) I don't! She's dressed like she works at a car rental place!
BETH:	What?
SUZANNE:	I like your pants. What colour would you call that?
BETH:	Khaki?
SUZANNE:	Yes. Khaki. You don't see that enough outside of the military.

> *GLENDA mouths "COMPLIMENT" to SUZANNE.*

	It's good. Easier to hide.
BETH:	Thank you. And I like your…whatever you would call that.
GLENDA:	I think it's called a muumuu.
SUZANNE:	It's a dress, thank you.
BETH:	Your earrings are very whimsical. Are those peacocks?
SUZANNE:	I believe so. And yours? Are they ball bearings? So fetching.
GLENDA:	(*Clapping to break the tension*) We all like what one another is wearing! Splendid! Shall we get Beth a refreshment? She's driven a long way. Beth, are you thirsty?

BETH:	I am, actually. I'd love some water.
GLENDA:	Here you go.

> *GLENDA pours from the pitcher and hands the glass to BETH.*

BETH:	This is water?
GLENDA:	It has water in it. Well, ice.

> *BETH takes a sip. Whatever it is, it's strong. She coughs.*

That'll be the rum. Maybe.

BETH:	Maybe?
GLENDA:	It may be rum.
BETH:	What do you mean it may be rum?
GLENDA:	We buy it from a local distillery. It comes in big unlabelled jugs.
BETH:	"Local distillery" isn't a euphemism for someone's bathtub, is it?
GLENDA:	I'm going to get you some chicken.
BETH:	I'm not hungry.
GLENDA:	But we have so much left over. Don't let Vera's death be in vain.

> *GLENDA exits to the house. She mouths "BE NICE" to SUZANNE as she passes. A long beat.*

SUZANNE:	Well, you made it one piece. Long drive.
BETH:	That it is. *(Beat.)* You know, I really don't want any chicken.
SUZANNE:	Just have a few bites, for your aunt.

BETH:	Fine.

Another long beat.

SUZANNE:	It's a nice summer.
BETH:	Mm-hm.
SUZANNE:	Has it been hot in the city?
BETH:	Yeah. Here?
SUZANNE:	Yeah. Been keeping well? You and the cat?
BETH:	Me and the cat are both fine, thanks.
SUZANNE:	Great. And how's the doctor thing going?
BETH:	The doctor thing. It's going well.
SUZANNE:	Good. You haven't lost any patients or anything? Is that rude to ask? I don't know.
BETH:	It's…No, I haven't.
SUZANNE:	Oh, that's good. Well done.

Beat.

BETH:	Aunt Glenda looks like she's lost weight.
SUZANNE:	Let me take your bag.

She takes the handle. BETH doesn't let go.

BETH:	That's okay. I've got it.
SUZANNE:	I'll help you.
BETH:	It's just one bag.
SUZANNE:	What, are you smuggling heroin? Why can't I take your bag?
BETH:	Well, you don't need to. You're not the bellhop.

SUZANNE: You're a guest.

BETH: I'm not a guest. I grew up here. I can carry my own bag, Mom.

SUZANNE: But I want to.

BETH: Why?

SUZANNE: I'm being nice.

BETH: That's okay.

SUZANNE: Let me be nice!

> *SUZANNE tries to pry up BETH's fingers.*

BETH: Ow! Mom!

SUZANNE: *(Holding up BETH's left hand)* Wait a minute. What is this?

BETH: My hand?

SUZANNE: No. I mean this. You were wearing a ring there until recently.

BETH: What are you talking about?

SUZANNE: Your ring finger. The skin is pale. Your hand is tanned but the ring left a pale circle behind where the sun didn't reach.

BETH: What are you, a forensic scientist?

SUZANNE: No, I've just met a lot of men in bars. What kind of ring do you wear on your left ring finger?!

BETH: Is that a rhetorical question?

SUZANNE: An engagement ring! *(Beat.)* Beth?

BETH: Mom—

GLENDA enters with a plate.

GLENDA: Ready to eat? *(Beat.)* Oh no, why the faces?

SUZANNE: Beth was engaged! Or is it "is engaged"?

BETH: All right, hang on—

GLENDA: What?

SUZANNE: *(Pointing to BETH's finger.)* Look!

GLENDA: What am I looking at?

SUZANNE: Nothing! That's what you're looking at!

GLENDA: What?!

SUZANNE: *(To BETH.)* Where is it?

BETH: Where's what?

SUZANNE: The ring!

GLENDA: What ring?

SUZANNE: *The* ring!

GLENDA: You have a ring?

BETH: No.

SUZANNE: Well, you did! What happened to it? And don't lie. I can tell.

GLENDA: I'm sorry, what did I miss?

SUZANNE: She was engaged!

GLENDA: Engaged! Beth?

BETH: *(To GLENDA.)* I don't want to talk about it.

GLENDA: Oh, she doesn't want to talk about it.

SUZANNE: So, there is something to talk about!

BETH: No, there isn't, because I just said I don't want to! Could we please change the subject?

SUZANNE: To what? What else could I possibly care about right now?

BETH: I don't know. I just got here. Maybe you could care about how I'm doing.

SUZANNE: I do care about that, but first I have questions. Like, what happened? Who was he, when did he give you a ring, why did he take it back and how many carats was it?!

BETH: I said I don't want to talk about it!

SUZANNE: Well, that's clear from the fact that this is the very first we're hearing of it!

BETH: Mom, could you ease up a bit? I just drove all day after working a twelve-hour shift at the hospital. I'm tired. I don't want to get into my relationship status right now!

GLENDA: Oh, Beth. Suzanne, we should let her rest.

SUZANNE: I'm sorry, your relationship status? What is your relationship status? I didn't know you had a relationship status. I thought your main relationship was with your cat!

BETH: Oh, my God!

SUZANNE: I'm your mother. How could you keep this from me?

BETH: This maybe rum isn't strong enough.

GLENDA: You want more?

BETH: I want a nap, and a shower.

SUZANNE: Answer me, Beth!

GLENDA: Suzanne.

BETH: Or else I may fall asleep right here in the dirt.

GLENDA: No, you won't. Come on. I've got fresh sheets
             on your bed.

SUZANNE: Where are you going? Who gave you the
             ring?

BETH: None of your business!

             GLENDA ushers BETH into the house.

SUZANNE: *(Calling after them.)* Did the cat give you the
             ring?

             BETH slams the door.

             End of scene.

Scene Three

A few hours later.

Lights up. SUZANNE and GLENDA play a game of Scrabble on the porch. There's a dish of strange candies on the table.

GLENDA: Fourteen, fifteen, sixteen points.

SUZANNE: That's not a word.

GLENDA: Sure it is.

SUZANNE: Nosy is not spelled with a zed.

GLENDA: Isn't it? Well, you would know.

SUZANNE: Oh, are we playing passive-aggressive Scrabble? No points. You spelled it wrong.

GLENDA: I will make another word.

SUZANNE watches as GLENDA lays down a different word.

SUZANNE: Stubborn has two "b"s. Do you have something you want to say?

GLENDA: Oh, you want my opinion?

SUZANNE: Do I have a choice?

GLENDA: You were not being nice.

SUZANNE: To Beth?

GLENDA: Who else? You promised you were going to be nice and then you came out with both guns blazing.

SUZANNE: Well, she wasn't exactly being nice herself.

GLENDA: How can you say that? She brought us these lovely candies from Toronto.

SUZANNE: They're terrible!

GLENDA: They're not that bad.

SUZANNE: Glenda, she kept it from me that she was engaged.

GLENDA: So what? Maybe she was going to tell you in her own time. You don't know what happened, Suzanne. Maybe it's something painful. Maybe he broke her heart.

SUZANNE: You think so?

GLENDA: I don't know, maybe. But you're never going to find out if you push her away. And I'm not just saying this for her sake, I'm saying it for mine. I really want to hear this story.

SUZANNE: Me too.

GLENDA: You've got to let her come to you.

SUZANNE: What if she never comes to me? You know she still holds a grudge about that time she confided in me about her crush on Danny Gillam and I accidentally told his mother.

GLENDA: She didn't confide in you. You read about it in her diary. And you didn't accidentally tell his mother, you sent her a letter.

SUZANNE: I was trying to help! *(Beat.)* I wasn't trying to push her away. I was a little angry she didn't even tell me she was engaged. That's a pretty big thing to leave out.

GLENDA: Well, we're keeping a whopper from her, too.

SUZANNE: That's different.

GLENDA: It's not that different.

SUZANNE: I'm doing that for you. I think we should tell her.

GLENDA: We will tell her. Later.

SUZANNE: You keep saying that. Later, when?

GLENDA: Later, later.

SUZANNE: Later is going to catch up to you, you know. Eventually, later arrives. You can live for today all you want but at some point there'll be a knock at the door and you know who will be standing on the other side? Later.

GLENDA: I know that.

SUZANNE: Do you? Because every time I try to talk about it, you say "not now."

GLENDA: Well, Suzanne, maybe I'm not ready. And, hey, why is the heat on me all of the sudden? We were talking about Beth and what a lousy daughter she is.

SUZANNE: What?

GLENDA: Keeping that secret from you.

SUZANNE: That was lousy.

GLENDA: It sure was. Boy, you should be mad about that.

SUZANNE: I am.

GLENDA: Well, I don't blame ya.

SUZANNE: Who would?

GLENDA: Kids.

SUZANNE: I know.

GLENDA: You give 'em everything you got and they give you nothing but heartache in return. Little jerks.

SUZANNE: You don't even have kids.

GLENDA: I'm just saying, I get why you'd be mad at her. *(Beat.)* Just, don't stay mad. Give her the benefit of the doubt. People keep secrets for a reason.

SUZANNE: Yes. All right. I know.

GLENDA: Don't chew your fingers. Have another candy.

SUZANNE: They're really terrible.

GLENDA: She'll come around and then she'll tell us why the engagement is off. I'm sure that too had a very good reason. Probably those pants.

SUZANNE: Why does she wear those pants?!

GLENDA: God bless her. At her age I was in pants so tight it took two people to get 'em on.

SUZANNE: And off, as I recall. *(Beat.)* I wish we'd kept those.

               BETH enters from the house in a night-gown.

GLENDA: Oh, she's up! Feeling better?

BETH: Yes, thank you.

GLENDA: Is the bed all right?

BETH: I spent last night on a sofa in the staff lounge. The bed is incredible.

GLENDA: Good. Well, now that you're up, I think your mom wants to say something to you.

SUZANNE:	Do I?
GLENDA:	Mm-hm. You do.
SUZANNE:	I don't think so.
GLENDA:	You must want to apologize for earlier. For being so pushy.
SUZANNE:	I wouldn't say I was pushy.
GLENDA:	For prying.
SUZANNE:	I don't think I pried.
GLENDA:	For sticking your big nose in your grown-up daughter's business without her invitation. *(Beat.)* Go on.
SUZANNE:	I'm sorry if I did that.
GLENDA:	You did do it.
SUZANNE:	I'm sorry that I did that.
BETH:	Really?
SUZANNE:	Yes.

Beat.

BETH:	Okay.
SUZANNE:	Okay?
BETH:	Yes.
SUZANNE:	Truce?
BETH:	Fine.

Beat.

SUZANNE:	Now do you want to talk about it?
BETH:	No.

BETH sits on the porch step. A long beat. GLENDA and SUZANNE look at her with hopeful faces.

Oh, fine! He's a doctor.

They crowd on the step with her.

GLENDA: Tell us everything!

SUZANNE: Use details.

BETH: His name is Barry.

SUZANNE: Barry? Like Manilow?

BETH: Like Anderson. Doctor Barry Anderson.

SUZANNE: How old is this guy?

BETH: My age.

SUZANNE: And someone named him Barry?

BETH: Are you going to let me tell the story?

SUZANNE: Yes, sorry. How'd you meet Barry?

BETH: In residency. I didn't really notice him at first, but we were working on the same unit and, over time, you know…

GLENDA: You started working on *his* unit.

BETH: Aunt Glenda, no. Don't say things like that.

GLENDA: I'm sorry.

BETH: But…yes, in a manner of speaking.

SUZANNE: Wait a minute, are you saying this was a casual hookup?

BETH: Well, initially.

SUZANNE: Atta girl!

BETH: Mom!

SUZANNE: No, I'm just surprised. How was it?

GLENDA: Suzanne! *(Beat. To BETH.)* But, seriously, what would you give him out of ten?

BETH: Okay, stop, before I change my mind about sharing.

> *SUZANNE and GLENDA make a lip zipping motion.*

So, yeah, we started...

SUZANNE: Hooking up.

BETH: Hooking up. You know, whenever we could fit it into our schedules. And after some time of that, we figured we'd might as well eat a meal before we...did that.

GLENDA: That's smart. Keep your strength up.

BETH: And if he stayed over, we'd have breakfast the next day. And sometimes on a Sunday go antiquing. About six months in we realized we were dating.

GLENDA: It kind of snuck up on you, huh?

BETH: Yeah, it did. And we were really happy together. We had lots in common. Both doctors, both liked breakfast... So, we dated for about a year and then he proposed, on our trip to Paris.

SUZANNE: Wait. Paris? Paris, Ontario, or Paris, France?

BETH: France. Why?

SUZANNE: Just, I didn't know you'd gone to Paris.

BETH: Didn't I tell you that?

SUZANNE: You didn't tell me any of this.

BETH: Oh. Sorry. Well, we went to Paris. And that's where he gave me the ring.

GLENDA: Oh, talk about that part! Or is it too painful?

BETH: No more painful than the rest. *(Beat.)* It was at the Eiffel Tower. *(About SUZANNE's expression.)* What?

SUZANNE: Nothing.

BETH: No. You made a face.

SUZANNE: I didn't—

BETH: You did.

SUZANNE: Did not. This is just my face.

BETH: What's wrong with the Eiffel Tower?

SUZANNE: Nothing. It's very beautiful.

BETH: Yes, it is.

SUZANNE: Not very imaginative.

BETH: What?

SUZANNE: I mean, you must have looked around and seen so many men kneeling you weren't sure which one was for you.

GLENDA: Suzanne.

BETH: No. He was the only one. And, he didn't even kneel.

GLENDA: He didn't kneel?

BETH: He has bad knees. *(To SUZANNE, before she can jump on this information.)* Don't say a word!

GLENDA: It sounds very romantic, either way, looking out over Paris. Were all the lights twinkling?

BETH: Not really. It was only 5:30. We had just had dinner.

SUZANNE: At 5:30, with Barry, who has bad knees? Oh come on! This guy is seventy if he's a day!

BETH: I've seen his driver's licence! He's thirty-seven!

SUZANNE: Are you sure you weren't looking at his year of birth?

BETH: Why do I tell you anything?

GLENDA: I think it all sounds beautiful, Beth.

BETH: Yeah, well, we're coming to the less beautiful part, now. Both Barry and I applied for a very prestigious fellowship in Montreal. And we agreed, if either of us got it, we'd move there. Well, last month, the letter came. And I got the fellowship.

SUZANNE
& GLENDA: Congratulations!

BETH: Thank you.

SUZANNE: That's great news!

BETH: Yes. (*Beat.*) Except Barry wasn't offered one. And, when it came down to it, he decided he didn't want to move after all. So he asked me to turn it down.

GLENDA: What?

SUZANNE: I hope you said, "Bite me, Barry"!

BETH: Well, I said something like that.

GLENDA: You two couldn't figure out a way to have a long-distance relationship, just for a year or two?

BETH: I thought we could've. He didn't agree.

GLENDA: I see. And you're sure this is what you want to do?

BETH: This fellowship is a once-in-a-lifetime opportunity.

GLENDA: So is love, Beth.

SUZANNE: Glenda, are you on drugs?! Of course she's taking the fellowship. Screw Barry! He'll meet a nice lady at bingo, or wherever he spends his time.

BETH: Mom!

SUZANNE: He didn't want to move? He didn't want a long-distance relationship? You know what he really didn't want? A wife that was more successful than him. And it's better to know that now. You did the right thing, Beth. And good on ya.

GLENDA: Suzanne, you don't know that. You've never even met him.

SUZANNE: Well, I know that people don't ask people they love to give up something that important. When you met Mark and he told you his life was here on this island, what did you do?

                 Beat.

GLENDA: I moved here.

SUZANNE: Of course you did. Because when you love someone you go where they are.

GLENDA: Well, I'm very sorry, Beth. He wasn't the one for you, then. It's as simple as that.

> *SUZANNE and GLENDA both touch BETH in a show of support.*

Do you want some maybe rum?

BETH: Maybe later.

GLENDA: How about some candy? *(About the dish of candies BETH gave them.)*

BETH: Those are bath beads. *(Beat. SUZANNE and GLENDA react to the fact they've each eaten at least one.)* No, I think what I need is to stop thinking about him, stop looking at his pictures, stop checking my phone to see if he's sent a message. And stop imagining a version of events where we both got that letter.

SUZANNE: Life is seldom that tidy.

GLENDA: Ain't that the truth.

BETH: Yeah.

> *BETH yawns. It sets off a chain reaction.*

GLENDA: Look at us three. I think we could all do with a good night's sleep.

SUZANNE: I sure could. If you're okay?

BETH: Yeah, I'm okay. I'm just going to enjoy the night air for a bit.

GLENDA: We're glad you're here.

BETH: I am too.

GLENDA: And tomorrow things will look a little brighter. They always do.

BETH: I'll be in in a bit.

SUZANNE
& GLENDA: Goodnight.

                   GLENDA and SUZANNE move towards the door. BETH takes out her phone. She unlocks the screen. SUZANNE and GLENDA look at her.

BETH: Oh, no. I'm not checking for messages from Barry. I've got some emails to write. Important...medical emails. *(Beat.)* No, I'm lying. I'm checking for messages from Barry. *(Looking at her phone.)* And...nothing.

GLENDA: Oh, honey. You miss him, huh?

BETH: I don't know. Do I? Or do I just want him to miss me?

SUZANNE: Well, are you sure he even knows how to use a computer at his age?

BETH: Go to bed!

                   SUZANNE and GLENDA exit to the house. BETH sits thinking.

                   End of scene.

Scene Four

>*Around noon, the next day.*
>
>*The sound of hammering comes from offstage, along with PATRICK singing to the radio. Lights up. BETH enters from the house. She wears the nightgown from the previous scene.*

BETH: Mom?

>*She looks towards the sound of PATRICK singing. She begins to clap for him. The music switches off. PATRICK enters, dressed in an undershirt and jeans, holding a water bottle.*

PATRICK: I'm sorry, I didn't know anyone was here. I knocked on the door—

BETH: No, I was enjoying the concert.

PATRICK: I'm sure that's not true. I got kicked out of the Christmas carolling club last year.

BETH: Well, their loss.

PATRICK: Thank you. *(He reaches for a handshake.)* I'm PATRICK. *(Taking in her attire.)* Oh. You're in a…night thingy. Wait, you must be Beth!

BETH: I am Beth.

PATRICK: Hi! I'm your neighbour. Your aunt's neighbour. And I'm fixing the shed. That's why I'm over there hammering, and singing badly.

BETH: Well, as long as you're not hammering badly.

PATRICK: Your aunt and your mom told me you'd be coming.

BETH: Did they? They didn't tell me about you.

PATRICK: Sorry about being half-naked. It's really hot up there.

BETH: No problem. You're fine. I mean, that's fine.

PATRICK: I guess you're kind of half-naked too, huh?

BETH: Oh, I normally wear more clothes. It's just that I was trying to make coffee and I couldn't figure out the machine, so I came out looking for my mom. I didn't expect there to be a man lurking around the yard. *(Beat.)* Not that you're lurking. That sounds so creepy. "Lurking." You're not lurking. You're just here. Just standing.

PATRICK: Uh-huh.

BETH: You must be new to the area. When I lived here the neighbour was a cranky old man who collected cans. I guess he probably died.

PATRICK: No, he didn't die. That's my dad.

BETH: Oh. I'm sorry.

PATRICK: It's okay. He is kind of cranky and he does collect cans, but only to make them into handicrafts. I moved in with him last year.

BETH: I didn't know he had any family.

PATRICK: Just me, and I grew up in Sudbury with my mom. But he needs more help these days. I suppose if I'd grown up here, I'd have met you.

BETH: Yeah. I mean, we'd have been neighbours.

PATRICK: We would have run into each other half-naked all the time.

BETH: Oh, God. I'm going to go get dressed.

PATRICK: No, don't be silly! You look great. And it's so hot out. Clothes would only make that worse. Seriously, don't change on my account. I don't mind that you're not wearing pants. In fact, I'd hate it if you were. Nope. I'm sorry. I've been out in the sun. I'm probably delirious.

BETH: What are you doing over there?

PATRICK: Reroofing. I got roped into it because I like your aunt's jam. The raspberry. I can't stop eating it.

BETH: Really?

PATRICK: I'm pretty sure I'm addicted. It's a slippery slope. First you're having a couple of a teaspoons a week on a piece of toast. Next thing you know it's midnight and you're eating it straight from the jar.

BETH: It is good.

PATRICK: Oh, it's the best. The best damn jam…ma'am. *(He clears his throat.)* I think I should have some water.

PATRICK drinks.

BETH: So raspberry jam, huh? That's your vice? You know, now that you live on the island, you should be eating the hawberry jelly.

PATRICK: I don't know if I could be trusted with it. *(Beat.)* Were you born on the island?

BETH: My mom moved here as soon as she found out she was pregnant. *(Beat.)* So, you're a handyman?

PATRICK: Oh, no. I'm—

GLENDA and SUZANNE enter from the side of the house. GLENDA has a box of donuts.

GLENDA: Beth! You're up!

BETH: Good morning.

SUZANNE: Morning.

GLENDA: Not in this time zone. Hey Patrick! I see you've met my niece. And you've lost your shirt.

BETH: Aunt Glenda.

PATRICK: I was getting hot.

SUZANNE: No one's complaining.

BETH: Mom!

GLENDA: We were going to introduce you two, but you've already met. So come, come. Sit! Visit! Look, we have fresh donuts!

BETH: Actually, I was just about to go get dressed.

PATRICK: And I should finish the roof.

GLENDA: Clothes, roofs, those can wait! Come on. How often do we have Beth here? Pull up a chair. Have a donut. Beth? You still like the ones with the rainbow sprinkles?

BETH: Of course not. I'm a grown woman.

GLENDA: Oh, so you don't want this?

            GLENDA holds out the rainbow sprinkle donut.

BETH: No.

GLENDA: Patrick? Donut?

PATRICK: Nah, I'm good.

GLENDA: Okay.

> *She puts a donut into his hand.*

PATRICK: …Thank you.

GLENDA: So! Have you two discovered all the things you have in common? Besides flat stomachs?

BETH: What?

GLENDA: Patrick and you.

BETH: Well, we're both mortified right now, if that's what you mean.

GLENDA: That's not what I mean. I mean, Patrick is also in the medical profession.

BETH: Is that right?

SUZANNE: He's a vet. He takes care of all the animals in Little Current.

BETH: You're kidding.

SUZANNE: *(To PATRICK.)* And Beth is a *real* doctor.

BETH: Mom!

SUZANNE: What? You are.

BETH: Vets are real doctors!

SUZANNE: Well, sure. Just not as real as the kind that work on people. I mean, let's face it, if you can't figure out what's wrong with one of your patients, you can't just take him out to the woodshed with a rifle.

PATRICK: We don't do that.

BETH: Of course you don't. She knows that. Mom, say sorry.

SUZANNE: Why? I'm not trying to discount what he does. He knows how to knock up a cow! I think that's great!

BETH: Patrick, I'm so sorry.

SUZANNE: You don't need to apologize for me.

PATRICK: It's fine. She's right. Veterinary college is a fraction of what you real doctors go through.

BETH: Don't be silly. I wouldn't know the first thing about knocking up a cow!

                   She looks to GLENDA to change the subject.

GLENDA: So, Patrick, tomorrow's the big day, huh? You ready?

PATRICK: Getting there.

BETH: The big day?

GLENDA: *(To BETH.)* PATRICK's fiancée is getting married tomorrow.

BETH: Oh. Congratulations!

PATRICK: Oh, no, no, not me. I'm not part of it.

BETH: I'm sorry?

PATRICK: She's marrying Chad.

GLENDA: Who is vegan.

BETH: Your fiancée…

PATRICK: Ex-fiancée…is marrying a vegan named Chad.

SUZANNE:	And Patrick is going.
BETH:	You're going to your ex-fiancée's wedding?
PATRICK:	Yeah.
BETH:	Isn't that going to be a little weird?
GLENDA:	It's gonna be very weird. But he's the salt of the earth, Patrick is.
PATRICK:	Truth is, I'm freaking out a little bit. I mean, I've never had to actually see her with *Chad*. I knew about *Chad*. I've thought about *Chad*. I've stared at *Chad* from across the grocery store. But I've never seen *Chad* and Tina. Tina and *Chad*!
BETH:	I hope you're not making the toast.
PATRICK:	Forgive me. It's—
BETH:	It's okay. I understand.
SUZANNE:	Oh, she does. She has a Tina.
GLENDA:	Named Barry.
BETH:	No, we don't need to talk about that.
SUZANNE:	Only difference is she dumped him. She wasn't left at the altar. *(PATRICK is about to object.)* Excuse me, near the altar.
GLENDA:	And he's a doctor, not a supervisor at the frozen yogurt store.
BETH:	Okay, I think that covers it.
SUZANNE:	You see, Beth got a very good job in Montreal and he didn't want to go.
BETH:	Mom.
GLENDA:	Probably because of his bad knees.

BETH: Aunt Glenda.

SUZANNE: He wasn't good enough for her.

GLENDA: I never liked him.

BETH: You never met him! And that's enough sharing, thank you.

SUZANNE: I'm done. I was just letting Patrick know that you're on the rebound just like him.

BETH: No! I'm not.

GLENDA: *(To PATRICK, sotto.)* Denial. It's normal.

SUZANNE: You know what you both need? Rebound sex. Do you know about rebound sex, Patrick?

BETH: *(To GLENDA.)* Give me that donut!

SUZANNE: Literally any partner will do.

BETH: Make it the whole box.

> *GLENDA passes BETH the donuts.*

SUZANNE: Are you listening, Beth?

BETH: I'm trying not to.

SUZANNE: *Cosmo.* You can borrow it. It's upstairs. Rebound sex is no longer considered taboo. In fact, it's considered very feminist. They put it on the cover.

BETH: Well, if it was on the cover of *Cosmo.*

SUZANNE: How did I raise such a prude? You know, everyone does it. Someone is doing it right now.

BETH: Okay! If everyone will excuse me, I think I'm going to go eat these in the closet. Patrick, it was a pleasure.

PATRICK: Pleasure was mine.

                BETH exits.

                Well, it's getting late. Better make hay while the sun shines.

GLENDA: Are you sure?

PATRICK: Yeah. Thanks for the donut.

GLENDA: Anytime.

                PATRICK exits. After a moment, the sound of hammering begins offstage.

                Look at him over there, working in this heat to help us out. Salt of the earth. I sure like him.

SUZANNE: Me too.

GLENDA: Shame about that business with Tina.

SUZANNE: Mm-hmm.

GLENDA: And now he has to go to her wedding alone.

SUZANNE: Shame.

GLENDA: Real shame. *(Beat.)* Are you thinking what I'm thinking?

SUZANNE: Oh, I think so.

GLENDA: So you're following my train of thought?

SUZANNE: I believe we got on at the same station.

GLENDA: All right then. We should get Beth to go as his date.

                Beat.

SUZANNE: What?

GLENDA: Isn't that what you were thinking?

SUZANNE: No.

GLENDA: Well, what were you thinking?

SUZANNE: That *I* should go as his date. But, now that I've thought of it, Beth and him makes more sense.

GLENDA: You didn't think of it, I thought of it!

SUZANNE: Well, once you said it, I started thinking about it.

GLENDA: You think she'd go?

SUZANNE: The girl who brought home every wounded animal in the neighbourhood? Of course she will. All we have to do is lay out the sob story about him being left at the altar, eating that cake alone, the dog, Tina being Satan in a dress...

GLENDA: She'll eat that up.

SUZANNE: She may be a little tightly wound, but she's got a soft heart.

GLENDA: She does. So that's the plan. We'll lay it on real thick at dinner tonight.

SUZANNE: All right.

GLENDA: Good. *(Beat)* You know, I'm proud of us. This is a good thing we're doing for Patrick.

SUZANNE: It is.

GLENDA: We're fine people, you know that?

SUZANNE: We are.

GLENDA: Kind, generous...

SUZANNE: Didn't you kick him out of the carolling club last year?

GLENDA: Yeah, he's a terrible singer.

They exit into the house.

End of scene.

Scene Five

The next day. Afternoon.

BETH enters from the house wearing one of SUZANNE's dresses. It's both short and low-cut. She carries a pair of high heeled shoes—also SUZANNE's—which she sets down on the porch.

BETH: Mom? *(She moves across the porch. She tugs the hem of the dress down. Doing this makes the neckline plunge lower. She tugs that up. The hem moves.)* Mom? This cannot possibly be the whole dress. Mom!

SUZANNE enters from the house. She's partially dressed for the wedding. Perhaps she's still putting on earrings or zipping something up.

SUZANNE: What are you hollering about?

BETH: This dress you gave me. Whose is it?

SUZANNE: It's mine.

BETH: It's scandalous!

SUZANNE: That's what I look for in a dress. Stop tugging it like that. You're pulling it down too much.

BETH: Too much? If I don't pull it down people will know the brand and size of underwear I have on. And, by the way, the only pair that worked with this dress do not offer a lot of coverage.

SUZANNE: That's why I don't wear underwear with it.

BETH: Oh God, Mom. Where do you wear this?

SUZANNE: I wear it all over. I last wore it to the theatre. We went to *The Best Little Whorehouse in Texas*.

BETH: Were you in the show?

> *GLENDA enters from the house holding a long, floral dress. She is also dressed for the wedding.*

GLENDA: Found it! *(She sees BETH.)* Holy shit. She can't wear that.

SUZANNE: Why not?

GLENDA: For starters, it breaks the biggest rule of dressing: boobs or legs. Never both. Here, Beth.

> *GLENDA tries to pull the dress down to cover more of BETH's legs. SUZANNE pulls it up.*

SUZANNE: I don't like that rule.

GLENDA: You don't like any rule. Nevertheless, the world needs rules or else it spins into chaos. War. Anarchy. Boobs and legs hanging out everywhere.

> *They continue pulling and pushing on BETH's dress.*

BETH: Stop it! Would you two get off me?

> *SUZANNE and GLENDA step back, holding up their hands.*

Thank you.

> *SUZANNE reaches back and tugs the dress up.*

Mom!

SUZANNE:	Sorry.
BETH:	I'm not wearing this. I'm not comfortable in it, and it does not say "I'm accompanying you to a wedding in a purely platonic manner."
GLENDA:	Noo. It says, "Pour me another mojito and meet me in the supply closet."
BETH:	Exactly.
SUZANNE:	All right. You take it off. I'll wear it.
GLENDA:	Try this one, Beth.
SUZANNE:	She's not wearing that one.
GLENDA:	Why not?
SUZANNE:	It looks like a tablecloth.
GLENDA:	Good eye! It was a tablecloth. I liked the print. I had it made into a dress.
BETH:	Are you serious?
GLENDA:	Yeah. That's why there's this gravy stain on the back.
SUZANNE:	She's not wearing the gravy dress.
GLENDA:	It's at the back!
SUZANNE:	Glenda, this is Northern Ontario. If she goes out wearing gravy she's going to be eaten by something.
GLENDA:	Fine. I've got another one upstairs that only has a cranberry stain on it.

They stare at her.

It was a big tablecloth.

BETH:	No offence, but I don't think I'd even like this as a tablecloth. Don't you have anything else? Mom? Maybe something you would wear to a funeral?
SUZANNE:	That is what I wear to funerals. No, we have nothing else. We have *(Referring to the dresses on BETH, herself and GLENDA.)* this, this, and that. How many fancy events do you think we get invited to? Here, try it with the shoes.
BETH:	Good idea. If I find people are staring at me I can distract them by breaking my legs. Are these even your size?
SUZANNE:	I was feeling optimistic. Come on, humour me.

BETH puts the shoes on.

GLENDA:	Wow.
SUZANNE:	She gets those legs from me.
GLENDA:	Still. So skimpy.
SUZANNE:	Who cares? Look at her!
GLENDA:	I'm looking at her. Everyone's going to be looking at her.
SUZANNE:	That's the point. *(To BETH.)* Live a little!
BETH:	I don't know. Maybe I could just wear my khaki pants and a nice blouse.
SUZANNE & GLENDA:	No!
BETH:	Why?
GLENDA:	Ooh! I know. I have a shawl!

GLENDA exits to the house.

BETH: Did it start out as curtains?

SUZANNE: Do you want to borrow a push-up bra?

BETH: I'm wearing a push-up bra.

SUZANNE: Oh.

> *GLENDA enters with a shawl and drapes it over BETH's shoulders.*

GLENDA: There. Now she's demure.

SUZANNE: Demure? What a horrible word. Take that off. She looks like a doily.

> *SUZANNE pulls the shawl off.*

GLENDA: A little mystery. Something to unwrap.

> *GLENDA puts the shawl back over BETH's shoulders.*

BETH: No one's going to be unwrapping anything!

> *Beat. SUZANNE pulls the shawl off.*

GLENDA: Suzanne.

> *PATRICK enters in a suit.*

PATRICK: Good evvvv—

> *PATRICK stops dead in his tracks, staring at BETH. Upon seeing his reaction, GLENDA chucks the shawl towards the house.*

GLENDA: Yeah, you don't need the shawl.

BETH: Hi, Patrick.

PATRICK: Hi. Wow. You look…very nice.

BETH: Thank you. And you do too.

PATRICK: That is some dress.

BETH: I think I should change.

PATRICK: Change? Why? Why would you change?

BETH: I mean, I don't know, is this dress appropriate?

PATRICK: I love it.

BETH: You do?

PATRICK: Yes. I do. And moreover, Tina will hate it. I mean, of course, wear whatever you like, but I sure wouldn't complain if you agreed to walk into the wedding on my arm looking exactly like you do right now.

BETH: Well...I... Really? *(Beat.)* Okay. Why the hell not?

SUZANNE: Atta girl.

PATRICK: Great. *(He forces himself to look away from BETH.)* You all look very nice.

SUZANNE: Thank you. You're not too shabby yourself. New suit?

PATRICK: Well, no, but it's the first time I'm wearing it out. It was my wedding suit.

BETH: You're wearing your wedding suit to your ex-fiancée's wedding?

PATRICK: Is that bad etiquette? I figured she insisted I buy it, she might as well see it on me once.

GLENDA: That's right. Let her see what she's passing up.

PATRICK: Does it look all right? I'm not much of a suit guy.

BETH:	You look very handsome.
PATRICK:	Well, I feel very uncomfortable.
GLENDA:	Perfect. So does Beth. *(Beat.)* Where's Sparky?
PATRICK:	Oh, he's at the groomer. We'll have to pick him up on the way.

GLENDA sits, hit by a wave of pain. No one but SUZANNE takes notice.

Are you all set, then?

BETH:	Yeah, I guess so.
SUZANNE:	You two run on ahead. I think we'll take a separate car.
BETH:	In case you want to leave early?
SUZANNE:	No, in case you want to leave early.
BETH:	Are you sure?
SUZANNE:	Yep. We'll see you there.
BETH:	All right. See you there. *(PATRICK holds out his arm for BETH. As they exit, she has a near miss on the shoes.)* Ho boy.
PATRICK:	I got ya.

They exit.

SUZANNE:	Talk to me.
GLENDA:	I'm fine.
SUZANNE:	I know that look.
GLENDA:	I just over-exerted myself looking for the dress.

SUZANNE: Have you told Doctor Jennings the pain is getting worse?

GLENDA: He said it would.

SUZANNE: ·   Can't they give you something?

GLENDA: I got something.

                GLENDA pulls a joint out of her evening bag.

SUZANNE: Is that a joint?

GLENDA: Shh! I don't want the neighbours knowing I'm a pothead.

SUZANNE: You're hardly a pothead. Did Dr. Jennings say it was okay?

GLENDA: He suggested it.

SUZANNE: Great. Well, light it up.

GLENDA: No!

SUZANNE: Why not?

GLENDA: It's for emergencies. I'm not about to become dependent on weed to get through my days.

SUZANNE: Lots of people smoke weed.

GLENDA: Yeah. Twenty-year-olds named Ty who work at the comic book store. Not nice, church-going ladies who sell jam.

SUZANNE: You went to church one time!

GLENDA: Suzanne, I'm serious. I'm not ready to be at that stage.

SUZANNE: What stage? The stage where you need a little something for the pain? Honey, there's nothing wrong with taking something. When you have a headache, you take a Tylenol. When you have…

GLENDA: Cancer?

SUZANNE: You take something stronger.

GLENDA: You should get going. You'll miss the bride's entrance.

SUZANNE: You're not coming?

GLENDA: No. I don't think so. I'm sure Deb will understand. I'm just not up to it.

SUZANNE: All right. *(She takes off her shoes.)* Then pass me that joint.

GLENDA: What are you doing?

SUZANNE: We're going to get high.

GLENDA: What are you doing? You've got to go to the wedding.

SUZANNE: Why?

GLENDA: Because. You love parties. You deserve a party.

SUZANNE: Babe, you are my party.

> *GLENDA picks the joint up. SUZANNE switches on the radio. A song like "Have You Ever Seen the Rain" by Creedence Clearwater Revival plays. GLENDA reaches out and takes her hand. They stay there a moment.*
>
> *End of Act One.*

ACT TWO

Scene One

That night, late.

BETH limps in on PATRICK's arm, holding her shoes. PATRICK holds a somewhat ragged bridal bouquet.

BETH: Ow.

PATRICK: You're doing great. Just a few more steps.

BETH: Okay. *(She takes a few more steps.)* Ow.

PATRICK: Here, here. Sit.

He leads her to the bench in the gazebo.

BETH: Thank you.

PATRICK: Elevate the injury.

BETH: Yes, I know.

PATRICK: Right. Yes. Sorry, Doctor.

BETH: I predicted this, you know. Those are not shoes, they're stilts.

PATRICK: Hey, you made it almost the whole night.

BETH: I'm so mortified.

PATRICK: Don't be. Hardly anyone saw.

BETH: Everyone saw! I skidded across the dance floor and crashed into the ice sculpture. It's probably already on the internet.

PATRICK: I'm just impressed you still managed to catch the bouquet.

BETH: I wasn't trying to catch it. I was trying to avoid getting hit by it.

PATRICK: She really hurled it at you, didn't she?

BETH: Like it was a hand grenade.

PATRICK: Well, I don't think she liked me showing up with a date.

BETH: No. Which, when you think about it, is a bit of a double standard. *(Beat.)* Ouch.

PATRICK: Here, let me take a look.

BETH: Oh…

PATRICK: What?

BETH: Well, it's just that…I'm not a golden retriever.

PATRICK: That's funny. May I? *(She nods. He takes her ankle.)* Does that hurt?

BETH: A little.

PATRICK: How about here?

BETH: Ow.

PATRICK: Can you wiggle your toes? *(She does.)* Good. And what about when I press like this? *(She groans.)* Okay. Well, I've got some bad news for you.

BETH: What?

PATRICK: You have heartworm. *(She laughs.)* Nah. It's just a sprain. I'm sure nothing's fractured. But, if you're worried, you can come by the clinic tomorrow and I'll X-ray you.

BETH: I'll take your word for it, Doctor.

PATRICK: Take a couple Advil before bed, baby it the next few days and you should be just fine. If not, we'll have to have you put down.

BETH: I'm sorry I made you leave the party early.

PATRICK: Nah, that's okay. Sparky was getting bored. They weren't playing any of his favourite songs.

BETH: You didn't get a chance to dance.

PATRICK: That is for the best.

BETH: Well, I didn't get a chance to dance and I'm a good dancer.

PATRICK: I know, I saw you with the ice sculpture.

BETH: What the hell was that supposed to be, anyway?

PATRICK: A portrait of Tina. It was a wedding gift from Chad.

BETH: It was?

PATRICK: It was pretty awesome.

BETH: I'm so sorry.

PATRICK: Apparently he carved it himself.

BETH: Oh my God, it keeps getting better.

PATRICK: King of romance, that guy.

BETH: I don't know. Hacking into her with an ice pick? That's not my idea of romance.

PATRICK: Oh no?

BETH: It wouldn't make me weak in the knees.

PATRICK: Well, what would?

BETH: I don't know. Not watching myself melt all over the linoleum.

PATRICK: How about flowers?

BETH: Nobody who works in a hospital likes flowers.

PATRICK: Chocolates? *(She shrugs.)* What then?

BETH: For me, it's not the showy stuff. That shed you're working on used to be my uncle's shop. He was fixing up this old Harley in there. He loved working on that bike. Then my aunt started making her jams and her hawberry jelly. Right away, people were lining up for it. She was thrilled, but it wasn't long before we started running out of space for her inventory in the house. We had jam jars everywhere except the bathroom. So, one day he took that old bike down to the roadside and put a for sale sign on it. Then he packed up all his tools and his workbench and he converted the shed into storage. When she saw it, she was furious. She told him to put it all back. That's what she's like, she never wants to be a bother to anyone. He refused. He told her he was bored of working on the bike and he'd been thinking of selling it for a while anyway. But I was there the day it was picked up and his eyes were nearly brimming over watching that Harley be loaded into someone else's truck. When I asked him why he did it, he said "because nothing matters more than her."

PATRICK: I never met him, but they sound like they were a great couple.

BETH:	They were. *(About the gazebo.)* He built this for her, you know. Their initials are carved right there. G and M.
PATRICK:	It's beautiful.

Beat.

BETH:	God, I want that.
PATRICK:	Yeah, me too.
BETH:	Instead, look at us. I got dumped by a guy named Barry with bad knees and you got left at the altar by an unattractive woman who works at the yogurt store.
PATRICK:	Near the altar. And, wait, unattractive?
BETH:	Oh.
PATRICK:	Is that what you said? You think Tina's unattractive?
BETH:	I didn't mean to say that.
PATRICK:	What about her is so unattractive?
BETH:	No, that just slipped out. I really didn't mean it. *(Beat.)* She's kind of horsey.
PATRICK:	Horsey?
BETH:	Yeah. Big nose, big teeth. Ugh, what is wrong with me? I'm being terrible!
PATRICK:	No. I mean, she's my ex, what do I care? Also, she threw a bouquet at you.
BETH:	Yeah, and it really hurt! There's something metal in there. *(Beat.)* How are you, anyway? Was that…okay for you?

PATRICK: It was weird, just like you all warned me it would be. I'd always imagined it, you know, when it was me she was marrying. I imagined the moment of seeing her for the first time in the church. The "Bridal Chorus" striking up: da da da da, and everyone turning to look at the bride. But when I finally saw her today— all in white, sunlight streaming through the stained glass, the music swelling—I didn't feel anything.

BETH: Really? Nothing?

PATRICK: Well, actually, not nothing. I felt sorry for vegan Chad. I mean, that whole wedding was our wedding. All the details were exactly what she'd planned with me, except there was a new guy playing the part of the groom.

BETH: Maybe he's better for the role? I know I don't really know her, but you two seem pretty different. I mean, you're nice and she... doesn't seem nice.

PATRICK: She's not that nice.

BETH: She's got a good pitching arm though.

PATRICK: She really did a number on me. We had everything planned out, and then, suddenly, I'm standing alone at this gaping chasm where my future had been. Everyone told me it would get better with time. And tonight I finally see they were right.

BETH: Well, I'm glad, Patrick. That gives me hope.

A long beat.

PATRICK: I wanted to thank you, by the way. For coming with me. And wearing that dress. If I didn't say so before, you look...

BETH: Like I'm wearing someone else's dress?

PATRICK: Beautiful.

BETH: Beautiful?

PATRICK: Breathtaking.

BETH: Oh. Thank you.

                 Another long beat. The tension builds.

PATRICK: I guess I should take you to bed, huh?

BETH: What?

PATRICK: No! I meant *get* you to bed. Your bed! Alone. I meant, I shouldn't keep you out. I didn't mean *that*. I did not mean *that*. Not at all. No.

BETH: Well, you don't have to be quite that emphatic about it.

PATRICK: Oh, no. Trust me, I'd love that! I mean, if we decided, jointly, to pursue something like that, and after an appropriate amount of time getting to know one another...You know, I could definitely...I mean, I would be very...

                 Beat. She stares at him.

                 This is why I work with animals. You throw humans at me and it all goes to hell. Maybe I should just shut up and walk you to the door.

BETH: I was kind of enjoying it. But it is getting late. And I'm probably going to need some help.

PATRICK: Of course.

                 He stands and gives her his arm.

BETH: Thank you.

                 They move slowly to the door.

Ow. I might need to be put down after all.

PATRICK: Almost there, Old Yeller. A few more steps.

At the door.

You made it. (*Beat.*) Thank you again, Beth. I had a really nice time.

BETH: Me too.

PATRICK: And you really do look beautiful. Okay. Well, goodnight.

BETH: Goodnight.

She leans to kiss him on the cheek. He leans to kiss her on the cheek at the same time. They end up nearly bumping noses.

PATRICK & BETH: Oh!

PATRICK/BETH: I was going to/I was trying to—

They try again. Same result.

BETH: I'm going to stand still.

PATRICK: Okay.

He leans to kiss her cheek, lingering a beat longer than necessary. She turns towards him. They kiss.

BETH: Goodnight.

PATRICK: Goodnight. (*He moves away, then returns.*) Are you going to manage the stairs okay?

BETH: Oh, um, yeah, I'll be fine.

PATRICK: Okay. (*Beat. He moves away and returns again.*) Don't need a spotter?

BETH: I think I've got it.

PATRICK: Okay. *(He moves away and returns again.)* You're sure?

BETH: Goodnight, Patrick.

PATRICK: Goodnight.

> *PATRICK moves away across the yard and exits. BETH opens the door, then hesitates. She looks towards him. She calls out.*

BETH: You know what, I might need help!

PATRICK: Coming!

> *He returns to her side. They share a look and then go into the house together.*
>
> *End of scene.*

Scene Two

The next day, almost noon.

GLENDA and SUZANNE come around the side of the house singing and giggling, arm in arm. They're dressed for church.

SUZANNE
& GLENDA: *(Singing)* "I'll be satisfied as long as I walk, let me walk close to thee. Just a closer walk with thee—"

BETH enters from the house.

BETH: Hello!

GLENDA: Hello! Suzanne, it's Beth.

SUZANNE: Hi, Beth.

BETH: What are you doing?

SUZANNE: Walking. What are you doing?

BETH: I've been here worrying about you. You didn't take your phone. I thought maybe Aunt Glenda started feeling worse overnight.

SUZANNE: No, no. She's feeling much better. Glenda, are you feeling much better? Beth wants to know.

GLENDA: Much better.

BETH: Oh, well, I'm glad to hear that. Where were you?

SUZANNE: Church.

BETH: Church?

SUZANNE: Yes, we go to church now.

BETH: Which church?

SUZANNE & GLENDA:	The pretty one!

> *They laugh at this.*

BETH:	Okay.
GLENDA:	We sat in a pew! Pew. Pew. *(To SUZANNE.)* Say that. It's funny. Pew.
SUZANNE:	Pew. Pew.
BETH:	Wait a minute. Are you drunk?
SUZANNE & GLENDA:	No.
BETH:	Are you sure?
GLENDA:	Positive. We are not drunk.

> *They laugh again.*

BETH:	Okay, what is going on?
SUZANNE:	Nothing's going on. What's going on with you?
BETH:	Touch your noses.
SUZANNE:	What?
BETH:	If you're not drunk, touch your noses.

> *GLENDA and SUZANNE reach out and touch one another's noses.*

GLENDA:	Boop.
BETH:	Your own noses! You ARE drunk!
SUZANNE:	We are not!
BETH:	You went to church like that? It's not even noon!

GLENDA:	*(To SUZANNE.)* We need to talk about Beth. When did she get so judgemental?
SUZANNE:	I know. What is up with that?
BETH:	I'm right here.

BETH crosses to them, limping.

GLENDA:	What happened to your foot?
BETH:	What happened to your pupils?
GLENDA:	You're limping.
BETH:	It's my ankle. It's just a sprain.
SUZANNE:	A sprain? Are you okay?
BETH:	I'm fine.
GLENDA:	Are you sure it's not broken? It doesn't look so good.
BETH:	It's not broken. Patrick examined it.
SUZANNE & GLENDA:	Ohh!
SUZANNE:	*(To GLENDA.)* She says Patrick examined it.
GLENDA:	I bet he did. What else do you think he examined?
SUZANNE:	Well, I don't know, but I've heard he's thorough.
BETH:	I'm still right here!
SUZANNE:	So you and Patrick played doctor, huh? That must have been fun.
BETH:	We didn't play doctor. We are doctors. And it wasn't like that!

GLENDA: And here I thought you'd only make it to first base.

SUZANNE: Tell me: does he have good hands? They look like good hands.

BETH: Mom!

SUZANNE: Clean, too. Have you noticed how clean his hands are?

BETH: Well, you'd be surprised how important that is to people in a doctor.

SUZANNE: Were they firm?

BETH: It was not like that! He's a medical professional. It was appropriately clinically detached.

SUZANNE: *(To GLENDA.)* Clinically detached? It didn't look too detached from that window up there.

GLENDA: No, it looked very attached.

BETH: What?

GLENDA: Mind you, I could barely see because your head was blocking most of my view.

SUZANNE: Well, I'm tall.

GLENDA: You're not tall, you just have big hair.

BETH: What did you say?

GLENDA: What?

BETH: You were watching us?!

GLENDA: How did you hear that?

BETH: I'm right here! I couldn't have not heard it if I tried!

GLENDA: *(To SUZANNE.)* I felt like we were talking really quietly.

BETH: You're serious? You actually spied on us from the window?? That is so creepy!

SUZANNE: We weren't spying! We were just watching! You know, in our defence, you don't tell us anything anymore.

BETH: Oh, is that your defence? Well, I figured telling you things would be repetitious, because you probably already read about most of them in my diary!

SUZANNE: You still keep a diary?

BETH: No!

SUZANNE: Well, then how could I read it?

BETH: I was being facetious! *(To GLENDA.)* Did you know she read my diary? She read it for years.

GLENDA: Oh. That's…terrible.

BETH: You wouldn't do that, would you? You wouldn't violate your daughter's privacy in such a shameless way.

GLENDA: I don't have a daughter.

BETH: Well, you wouldn't read anybody's diary. Would you? Aunt Glenda? *(Beat.)* Oh my God, you read it too!

SUZANNE: *(To GLENDA.)* Stay calm.

BETH: Aunt Glenda?

SUZANNE: Don't answer. They can't make you answer.

GLENDA: She looks really mad.

SUZANNE: Plead the fifth.

GLENDA: I think that's an American thing.

BETH: Look me in the eye.

GLENDA: I'm no good at this.

BETH: You read it? You read it, didn't you? Did you?

GLENDA: Avidly. *(Beat.)* I'm so sorry. Beth, I'm really sorry. It was a terrible thing to do! And I regret it. But…can you just tell me one thing? What ended up happening with Christy and Steve? Did they make up after prom?

BETH: Boundaries! Do boundaries mean anything to anyone in this house?! Don't answer that. I know the answer.

GLENDA: Is it "no"?

BETH: Yes, it's no! I used to think you and I were close, that you were even on my side. But now I see it as it's always been. The two of you, thick as thieves. And who is on my side? No one. Not since Uncle Mark died.

             BETH limps across the yard and sits on the bench.

SUZANNE: Shit.

GLENDA: Ouch.

SUZANNE: She didn't mean that.

GLENDA: No, she did. *(Beat.)* We really are horrible. We're not fine people. We're bad people.

SUZANNE: We're not bad people. We just make bad choices.

GLENDA: We need to apologize.

SUZANNE and GLENDA cross to BETH.

BETH: Please just leave me alone.

GLENDA: We're sorry.

BETH: I don't want to talk to you.

SUZANNE: Really sorry. We should not have spied on you and Patrick or taken pictures of you without your knowledge.

BETH: What?

GLENDA: For your wedding scrapbook. Just in case.

BETH: You took pictures?

SUZANNE: Yes. They probably won't turn out. It was dark and the angle wasn't great. And I'm telling you because you're right. We crossed a boundary. And we've done that a lot.

BETH: Is there anything else? Video?

SUZANNE: No.

BETH: Did you wiretap my bedroom?

SUZANNE: No.

BETH: Did you follow us upstairs?

SUZANNE: You went upstairs?

GLENDA: *(To SUZANNE.)* I told you we went to bed too early!

SUZANNE: No, we didn't follow you.

BETH: Well, small mercies.

SUZANNE: We're sorry. *(Beat.)* You went upstairs? Did he…stay?

BETH: None of your business.

SUZANNE: I just want to know if—

BETH: You just want to know everything! So you can control everything! Because God forbid I have my own life—

SUZANNE: That's not true—

BETH: Yes it is, Mom! I'm not answering any more questions. In fact, I've got some questions for you. Number one: what the hell is going on? And don't tell me nothing. You've both been acting strange since I got here, and you're acting stranger than ever today. Something is up. Now tell me what it is.

                    A long beat.

SUZANNE: We're high.

GLENDA: Suzanne.

SUZANNE: High as a pair of kites.

BETH: High? What do you mean high?

SUZANNE: Stoned. Baked. Wasted.

BETH: Like on drugs?!

SUZANNE: Marijuana.

GLENDA: Suzanne.

SUZANNE: As suggested by Glenda's oncologist.

GLENDA: Suzanne!

BETH: What?

SUZANNE: *(To GLENDA.)* We're already apologizing. Might as well get it all out.

BETH: Oncologist—

SUZANNE: Cancer doctor.

BETH: I know what an oncologist is! But why would you have an oncologist? You don't have cancer. *(Beat.)* You don't have cancer.

GLENDA: Beth.

BETH: Where? What kind?

GLENDA: Pancreatic.

A long beat.

BETH: When were you diagnosed?

GLENDA: Seven months ago.

BETH: Oh my God.

GLENDA: Beth.

BETH exits.

End of scene.

Scene Three

Late that evening.

GLENDA and SUZANNE are on the porch. SUZANNE is pacing, speaking on the phone.

SUZANNE: She's been gone for over eight hours, Bill. And she left her phone here. Her car? Well, it's a...sort of a stuffy-looking sedan. I don't know what make or model. Something a doctor would drive! Probably a Volvo! Well, I'm yelling at you because my only child is missing! Can't you send a car out to look for her? I don't care about it's only been eight hours, Bill. This is my kid we're talking about here. Mine. All right then. Call me if you hear anything. *(She hangs up.)* Well, I got Barney Fife on the case.

GLENDA: Good. Maybe we should go back out.

SUZANNE: We drove all over. And what if she comes back while we're gone?

GLENDA: Right.

SUZANNE: She's just mad. She's just cooling off. Right? She's sitting somewhere in her car. She's not lost in the bush.

GLENDA: Of course she's not. She knows better.

SUZANNE: So did Mark.

GLENDA: Suzanne, if you let your mind wander down that path you'll never get it back. And let me tell you, if something bad happened to her, you'd already know. You'd feel it.

SUZANNE: Did you?

GLENDA: Yes. I did. When he didn't come home that day...when it was dark and he still wasn't here, I had this...I don't know...I just knew. It was a feeling. A dark, suffocating feeling—like someone dropped a heavy net over me. And I knew we wouldn't find him alive.

SUZANNE: I remember that like it was yesterday. All those people out walking shoulder to shoulder. You never told me about your feeling.

GLENDA: I never told anyone. I never wanted to admit that I had no hope. Everyone else seemed to have so much. Who knew the bush better than Mark? No one thought anything bad could've happened to him out there. The point is, I don't feel that now. I don't feel that about Beth. She's okay, and she'll be back soon. Totally safe.

SUZANNE: Well, good, because I'm going to kill her when she gets back.

GLENDA: I'm sorry, Suzanne. This is all my fault.

SUZANNE: No, it's not.

GLENDA: We made her mad spying on her, but we broke her heart keeping this from her—and that was my doing.

SUZANNE: I don't think that's what broke her heart. She's in medicine. She knows the prognosis for pancreatic cancer. And you know what you mean to her. She didn't mean what she said.

GLENDA: She didn't mean what she said about you either.

SUZANNE: Oh yes she did. Look at the evidence. She's done everything she can to keep me out of her life. She's had whole fiancés I didn't know about.

GLENDA: Maybe that's normal.

SUZANNE: It's not normal. Your mother is the first person you tell when you get engaged. Then you plan a shopping date and you go pick out a wedding gown together. That's what you do. Unless you can't stand your mother. *(Beat.)* If I ask you something, will you tell me the truth?

GLENDA: No. I love you too much.

SUZANNE: I'm serious. I want to know. Do you think I smothered her?

GLENDA: Like it was an Olympic sport.

SUZANNE: Really?

GLENDA: Yes. But don't beat yourself up about it. God, Suzanne, you did your best. You were practically a kid yourself. You had a life, you had plans, and you gave them all up to come up here and give her a home.

SUZANNE: Your home.

GLENDA: It was barely a home until you two arrived. You gave Mark and me something we weren't able to have ourselves. A little one to watch grow. And she's a great kid. If I could've had my own and if I could guarantee they'd all turn out like Beth, I'd have had a dozen. And I know Mark felt the same way.

SUZANNE: He treated her like his own daughter.

GLENDA: That's how he saw her.

SUZANNE: You know, he's the only reason I never felt guilty about her not having her dad around. I asked her once if she wanted to try and find him. I'd have helped her. But she said she never thought much about him. I think that's because she wasn't missing a dad.

GLENDA: He'd have loved knowing that.

SUZANNE: He was a good man. Still, I can't believe he was her favourite.

GLENDA: Sure. He let her do whatever she wanted. He never criticized or disciplined her.

SUZANNE: Well, of course he didn't. He was a man. They don't do it because they know we will. You don't see roosters sitting on eggs, do you?

GLENDA: Don't start with the rooster again.

SUZANNE: I don't think I smothered her. I resent that word. I *mothered* her. It's different. So sometimes maybe I mothered her too hard... and she couldn't exactly breathe. Oh God, I smothered her. That's why we're not close, isn't it? I'm Mommy Dearest.

GLENDA: You're not Mommy Dearest. You're not even tidy.

SUZANNE: No, I mean it. I'm controlling. I always was. No one ever told me it was going to be so terrifying. Loving someone that much. It was one thing when she was little. I could keep her safe. But how was I supposed to send her out there, into the world? When I just wanted to grab onto her and say, "Don't go! You don't need all that. Just stay here! Just let me keep you!" God, that's sick, isn't it?

GLENDA: No. When you love someone, you want them where you are.

SUZANNE: She was so small.

GLENDA: I know. But, honey, she's not small anymore. She's big and she's smart and she's making a hell of a life for herself. I'd say that's proof you did a great job.

SUZANNE looks out towards the road.

SUZANNE: God, where is she?

GLENDA hugs SUZANNE. After a moment, BETH enters, carrying medical journals.

BETH: Hi.

SUZANNE
& GLENDA: Beth!

SUZANNE: Where've you been? You scared the hell out of us!

GLENDA: Your mother called the police!

BETH: I was over at McLean's Mountain lookout, eating poutine.

SUZANNE: All this time?

GLENDA: How much poutine did you have?

BETH: Well, the poutine only lasted about twenty minutes, but that's where I've been.

SUZANNE: Thank God you're safe.

BETH: I'm sorry I worried you.

SUZANNE: You didn't take your phone.

BETH: I know. I realized that as soon as I got in the car, but I'd made such a dramatic exit I couldn't come back and get it.

GLENDA: I didn't know you knew where the lookout was.

BETH: Uncle Mark took me there tobogganing. Most of those times you thought he was taking me over to Gordon's Park to see the northern lights? We were going tobogganing at the lookout.

GLENDA: He lied to us?

BETH: Sometimes we'd actually go to Gordon's Park. Sometimes you couldn't see the lights. Then we'd be glad we brought our toboggans along so the trip wasn't a waste.

SUZANNE: Did he put a helmet on you, at least?

BETH: Nope. Not once.

SUZANNE: *(To GLENDA.)* Rooster.

BETH: It was fun. I was remembering it when I was up there today. I was also going through these medical journals.

SUZANNE: I could've lent you a *Cosmo*.

BETH: There are some promising new cancer trials.

GLENDA: Oh.

BETH: There's one in particular, at Princess Margaret. You could stay at my place in the city. I haven't sold it yet.

GLENDA: Beth—

BETH: I don't know if they're still taking patients, but I could make some calls—

GLENDA: Beth, I decided…My treatment plan, it's only to control pain.

BETH: I understand, but there are protocols that can prolong life, in some cases months, and new trials all the time—

GLENDA: I don't want to go to Princess Margaret. I appreciate it, Beth, I do. But I don't want to go to the city.

BETH: I can't imagine you're getting the best possible care out here.

SUZANNE: Glenda, maybe she's right.

GLENDA: The city isn't my home anymore.

SUZANNE: You could get used to it again.

GLENDA: No, I couldn't. It's funny…When I came here as a newlywed, I hated it. I thought I'd made the biggest mistake of my life. I didn't know anyone and there was nothing here. None of my favourite stores or restaurants. Barely any stores or restaurants at all, back then. One night Mark and I had this blowout fight. I said, "That's it!" I threw my things in a suitcase, got in the car and told him I was leaving. Going back to the city, where I could get a decent calzone.

BETH: You left?

GLENDA: I tried. Turns out my getaway was poorly timed. I reached the swing bridge at exactly 7:00 pm, just as they were opening it to let the boats through. Got stuck in a lineup of cars waiting to cross. By the time the bridge was closed again, Mark was standing outside the driver side door, hat in his hands, begging me not to go. Call me crazy, but I believe the island wanted me here. With him. I never tried to leave again and I never want to.

BETH: Okay, then you stay and I'll find some way to get the medicine to you.

GLENDA: Quality.

BETH: What?

GLENDA: Quality of life. Not quantity. That's the choice I made. I did the chemotherapy. At the beginning. I'd spend a week sick and then a week recovering and about the time I started to feel human again, it was time for another round. However much time I get, that's not what I want it to be.

BETH: I see. *(A long beat.)* When were you going to tell me?

GLENDA: After this visit.

SUZANNE: Beth, I know you're hurt, but she was protecting you.

GLENDA: No. I was protecting myself. From how you'd treat me. From how, even in happy moments, I'd see a degree of sorrow in your eyes and that would make it harder for me to pretend my life is still normal. Because, since I got sick, it's hard for me to take things for granted. That's what separates people that are dying from everyone else. You're not looking up at a full moon wondering if it'll be your last. You're probably not looking at it at all. But me? Everything could be my last. My last full moon, the last time I see a monarch butterfly, the last time I hear Van Morrison sing "Brown Eyed Girl." Isn't that the cruellest joke? I can't just enjoy a song anymore without thinking about all the times I heard it before and wishing I could go back to any one of them. Be anywhere in the timeline of my life but where I am. At the end. So, I didn't want to tell you because, if I'm lucky, I get a couple minutes a day where I forget and I take things for granted, just like everyone else. Like the way the air smells tonight. Did you notice it? I didn't. Not until just now. It smells like summer—like flowers and dew on the grass. Last year, I sat out here nearly every evening and breathed all of that in without noticing it. *(Beat.) That* was my last summer.

SUZANNE: That's the first time I've heard you say it. That you're dying.

GLENDA: Yeah. Well, it's not my favourite subject.

All three draw close.

End of scene.

Scene Four

A few days later, midday.

*SUZANNE is on the porch. BETH enters
with her suitcase and a garment bag.*

SUZANNE: All set?

BETH: I think so.

SUZANNE: Do you want some help with that?

BETH: I've got it.

SUZANNE: Okay.

BETH: That visit went fast, didn't it?

SUZANNE: Really fast. I'm glad you came.

BETH: Me too.

SUZANNE: Oh, before I forget. *(SUZANNE hands BETH
              the photographs of her and PATRICK.)* Those are
              yours.

BETH: You printed them?

SUZANNE: I almost had them made into a calendar. But,
              no, I printed them in case you want them and
              then I erased my copies.

              BETH flips through the photos.

BETH: They're all of your head.

SUZANNE: Not the last one.

              *BETH looks at the last photo and smiles.
              She puts the photos away.*

BETH: You sure you don't mind me taking this
              dress?

SUZANNE: Nah. I think it's about time I passed the torch.

BETH: I might have the hem let out.

SUZANNE: Don't you dare.

> *GLENDA enters with a huge stack of Tupperware dishes and a bag full of groceries.*

GLENDA: Do you think I should get the big cooler from the basement? Does your car have air conditioning?

BETH: Aunt Glenda, what is all that?

GLENDA: The goat cheese might not keep.

BETH: Is that all food? Who is all of that for?

GLENDA: It's for you.

BETH: What am I going to do with it? I'm headed to Montreal as soon as I get back.

GLENDA: They don't eat in Montreal?

SUZANNE: Glenda, she can go to the grocery store.

GLENDA: This is local goat cheese.

SUZANNE: I'm sure they have goat cheese in Montreal.

GLENDA: Do they have goat cheese so fresh that if you look over that hill you can see the goat it's from? Trust me, this is better than anything they have in Montreal. And this corn is fresh. I picked it myself.

SUZANNE: No, you didn't.

GLENDA: Well, I picked it *up* myself. If you buy corn from a grocery store, it's been on a truck for three days. This corn is better.

SUZANNE: She's not a college student, she doesn't need us to send her home with a hamper. Some would say that's smothering her.

GLENDA: Right. Okay. Well, I just thought—

BETH: I'll take it. *(She picks up the grocery bag. Beat.)* I keep thinking I should stay.

GLENDA: We've been over this.

BETH: I can ask to start in Montreal later.

GLENDA: Absolutely not. Get your perky butt in that car.

BETH: If I explain the situation—

GLENDA: You're going. That's final. It's my dying wish.

SUZANNE: You know you can't make everything your dying wish. This morning you said it was your dying wish that I give you the last piece of bacon.

GLENDA: Oh, excuse me. Well, when you're dying, I'll let you have the last piece of bacon. *(To BETH.)* All right, go on with ya. Let's get this over with, before I get weepy.

            PATRICK enters with a newspaper.

SUZANNE: Patrick.

PATRICK: Just bringing your newspaper back.

SUZANNE: We already have our newspaper.

PATRICK: Yeah. This is my newspaper. I just wanted an excuse to come over.

GLENDA: Beth's leaving.

PATRICK: I know.

GLENDA: Aw, you came to say goodbye.

PATRICK: Uh. Yes. I guess I did.

GLENDA: Aw.

SUZANNE: Glenda, you want to help me with these things?

GLENDA: But then we'll miss Patrick saying goodbye to Beth.

SUZANNE: That's the point.

GLENDA: Oh.

> *SUZANNE takes the suitcase and groceries from BETH. She and GLENDA exit towards the driveway.*

PATRICK: So, you're off then? Back to the big city?

BETH: Yeah, I'm afraid so. I'll be back in a couple of months. I'll have a few days off.

PATRICK: Oh. Good. That'll be good.

BETH: Yeah.

PATRICK: Or, you know, you could stay.

BETH: I tried. They won't let me. We've been arguing about it.

PATRICK: Well, once-in-a-lifetime opportunity, I guess.

BETH: It is. Listen, I'm sorry. The last few days have been—

PATRICK: You don't need to apologize. I understand.

BETH: I just wish we had more time. And now I'm moving to Montreal.

PATRICK: It's not that far, you know. There's six flights a day out of Sudbury. I looked it up.

BETH: You'd want to come visit?

PATRICK: If that's where you're going to be, yeah.

BETH takes PATRICK's hand.

BETH: Will you do something else for me? Will you check in on them? I feel so useless so far away.

PATRICK: Of course.

BETH: You'll tell me how they're really doing? Because you know they'll only tell me the good stuff.

PATRICK: I'll report every night, if you want.

BETH: And pay special attention to my mom, okay? Make sure she's not burning out. I know she'll be so focused on my aunt she'll forget to take care of herself.

PATRICK: I will.

BETH: Thank you.

PATRICK: Well, I won't keep you. I just wanted to see you one more time before you left.

They kiss.

BETH: Let's talk soon, okay?

PATRICK: We will. We will.

PATRICK exits. BETH stares after him. SUZANNE enters. She, too, stares after PATRICK.

SUZANNE: Everything okay?

BETH: Yeah.

SUZANNE: Would it be interfering for me to say I like him?

BETH: No, because I like him too.

SUZANNE: And would it be interfering for me to observe that you two would have beautiful babies?

BETH: Yes.

GLENDA enters.

GLENDA: All packed up. Your rear driver's side tire looks a little low. You should add some air before you get on the highway.

BETH: All right.

SUZANNE: Well, I guess we shouldn't keep you. You don't want to be driving in the dark. You've got everything?

BETH: I think so.

SUZANNE: Call us when you get in, so we know you're safe.

BETH: I will.

BETH and SUZANNE hug.

Look, the next little while will be hectic, but you'll phone me if…if you need to. Right?

SUZANNE: Of course.

BETH: Okay.

BETH turns to GLENDA.

GLENDA: Bring it in.

GLENDA and BETH hug. Both hold on just a little longer than is normal.

BETH: Okay. I'm off. Goodbye.

BETH exits.

SUZANNE
& GLENDA: Goodbye.

SUZANNE and GLENDA watch BETH go. The sound of a car pulling out. SUZANNE busies herself pruning the flowers. There is silence awhile.

SUZANNE: The hydrangea have done well this year.

GLENDA: Mm-hm.

SUZANNE: They've always been my favourite. *(Beat.)* Hey, you'll never guess who I ran into at the garden centre.

GLENDA: Walt Kelly?

SUZANNE: How'd you guess?

GLENDA: He works there.

SUZANNE: Well, you'll never guess what he told me. He's moving to Espanola.

GLENDA: You're kidding. To be with Andrea?

SUZANNE: They're going to build a house there. She's got all this land. Used to be a dairy farm.

GLENDA: Wow. He's lived here his whole life.

SUZANNE: Must be love.

GLENDA: Must be. Well, good for them.

SUZANNE: Good for them.

Beat.

GLENDA: I think I might go to church later. For the evening service.

SUZANNE: You want company?

GLENDA: You don't have to.

SUZANNE: I don't mind.

GLENDA: Yes, you do. You hate church.

SUZANNE: I don't hate church.

GLENDA: You're like bringing a toddler. Next time I'm going to give you a box of raisins to keep you from squirming.

SUZANNE: Well, it's an awful lot of talking. And the seats are so uncomfortable.

GLENDA: Pews.

SUZANNE: Why do you go?

GLENDA: I like it. It's peaceful. And they believe there's life after death.

SUZANNE: Well, I don't mind going with you.

GLENDA: All right.

SUZANNE: You think we should've let her stay?

GLENDA: No.

SUZANNE: She wanted to.

GLENDA: She lost a fiancé to take that fellowship. I certainly can't have her pass it up for me.

SUZANNE: There will be other fellowships.

GLENDA: No. And I don't want to hear another word about it.

SUZANNE: Okay.

GLENDA: Speaking of cows—

SUZANNE: We weren't speaking of cows.

GLENDA: We were a minute ago.

SUZANNE: When?

GLENDA: When you said Andrea's property used to be a dairy farm.

SUZANNE: Well, you can't do a segue from a minute ago.

GLENDA: I'm dying. I can do whatever the hell I want.

SUZANNE: All right, what about the cows?

GLENDA: Kendall Cranford phoned over here today.

SUZANNE: What? What for?

GLENDA: For you.

SUZANNE: No, he didn't.

GLENDA: Said he missed you at Tina and Chad's wedding. He'd been hoping to see you there.

SUZANNE: What the hell for?

GLENDA: To continue his lecture about Holsteins, I guess.

SUZANNE: Ugh.

GLENDA: I don't know, he just had his hip replaced, maybe he wants to try it out. I didn't ask. But I left his number by the phone.

SUZANNE: Well, I'm not going to call him.

GLENDA: Why not?

SUZANNE: I'm busy.

GLENDA: You're not busy. You're like the least busy person I know. You should call him.

SUZANNE: Why are you suddenly so interested in me talking to Kendall Cranford?

GLENDA: I don't know, I just want you to keep your mind open. You might want some company.

SUZANNE: I don't need company. I've got you.

GLENDA: Call him.

SUZANNE: I'm not going to call him.

GLENDA: It's my dying wish.

SUZANNE: Glenda.

GLENDA: I mean it.

SUZANNE: Fine, I'll call him. You know, you're out of control. *(Beat.)* You think she remembered to fill that tire?

GLENDA: It wasn't that flat. It'll get her home.

> *They turn to the sound of a car pulling in, then a car door. BETH enters.*

BETH: The swing bridge was open.

GLENDA: What?

BETH: Bad timing. I got there at 12:01.

GLENDA: Beth.

BETH: There was a long lineup, so I just gave up and came back.

GLENDA: It'll be back down in a few minutes.

BETH: I don't think the island wants me to go. *(Beat.)* And, I don't want to go. The city's not my home either. This is. You are. And I know you're about to say I can't stay, but I'd like to remind you that I'm a grown woman and a doctor and I spent nearly a decade of my life in higher education, so I can make my own decisions. I don't want to be in Montreal. I don't care about the fellowship. I want to be where you are for as long as you're here.

GLENDA: Beth.

BETH: Where both of you are. That's my decision. *(Beat.)* Anyway...I think I'll take this newspaper back to Patrick. Then maybe the three of us can go for a late lunch in town?

GLENDA: I'd like that.

BETH: Good.

> *BETH picks up the newspaper and exits.*

SUZANNE: She's a great kid.

GLENDA: The very best. *(Beat. SUZANNE goes back to pruning.)* I've been thinking.

SUZANNE: Oh?

GLENDA: About how I haven't been facing this thing head on very well.

SUZANNE: You've been doing great.

GLENDA: So, I made some plans. For my...you know. My funeral.

SUZANNE: Oh.

GLENDA: Here.

> *GLENDA takes a piece of paper from her pocket and hands it to SUZANNE. They sit together.*

SUZANNE: Doves?

GLENDA: White ones. Not grey. If you can't get white, butterflies.

SUZANNE: That's not how you spell "Ave Maria." *(Reading further.)* Glenda, I'm not going to be able to get cannons.

GLENDA: Well, not with that attitude.

SUZANNE: *(Folding up the paper and putting it away.)* All right. I'll do my best.

GLENDA: Thank you. And by the way, when my time comes, don't go giving any speeches about how I would've wanted people to be happy.

SUZANNE: What?

GLENDA: I hate when people say that. "So and so would've wanted us to be happy." I don't want you to be happy. I want you to be bereft. It's my funeral. It's not Mardi Gras.

SUZANNE: Noted.

GLENDA: So now we've discussed it we can move on. Okay?

SUZANNE: Okay.

GLENDA: Good.

> *GLENDA switches the radio on. A song like "Brown Eyed Girl" plays.*

I love this song.

*She reaches out for SUZANNE's hand.
They sit.*

End of play.

Glossary / Background Information

Manitoulin Island, located in Lake Huron within the provincial boundary of Ontario, is the world's largest freshwater island. It sits on the traditional land of the Anishinaabe peoples. The name "Manitoulin" is the anglicized form of the Ojibwe *Manidoowaaling*, meaning "cave of the spirit." A place of abundant natural beauty, the island has over 100 inland lakes, some of which have their own islands, and four major river systems. Due to glacier erosion, the island also features areas of smooth, exposed bedrock.

Little Current, located on the northeast side, is the largest settlement on Manitoulin Island. Its economy includes agriculture and tourism. It is home to local businesses and notably absent of most large retail and restaurant chains.

The Little Current Swing Bridge carries Highway 6 across a narrow channel and forms the only land access from Little Goat Island to Manitoulin Island. The bridge stays in the closed position to allow the passage of road traffic except for at the top of each daylight hour when it opens for fifteen minutes to allow boats through. During this fifteen-minute period, cars can neither enter nor leave the island.

Hawberries are the bright red fruit of the hawthorn tree, which grows on Manitoulin Island.

The Manitoulin Expositor is the local newspaper of Little Current and is published weekly.

McLean's Mountain Lookout offers an elevated view of Little Current and the north channel of Lake Huron.

The Princess Margaret Cancer Centre in Toronto is a facility dedicated entirely to cancer research, education and treatment. It is recognized as a world leader in this field.